Street by Street

TOR...

BRIXHAM, NEWTON ABBOT, PAIGNTON, TEIGNMOUTH, TORQUAY, TOTNES

Ashburton, Babbacombe, Bishopsteignton, Bovey Tracey, Buckfastleigh, Dartmouth, Dawlish, Galmpton, Goodrington, Ipplepen, Kingsbridge, Kingskerswell, Kingsteignton, Marldon, Salcombe, Stoke Gabriel

3rd edition May 2009
© AA Media Limited 2009

Original edition printed May 2001

 This product includes map data licensed from Ordnance Survey® with the permission of the Controller of Her Majesty's Stationery Office. © Crown copyright 2009. All rights reserved. Licence number 100021153.

The copyright in all PAF is owned by Royal Mail Group plc.

 Information on fixed speed camera locations provided by RoadPilot © 2009 RoadPilot® Driving Technology.

Published by AA Publishing (a trading name of AA Media Limited, whose registered office is Fanum House, Basing View, Basingstoke, Hampshire RG21 4EA. Registered number 06112600).

Produced by the Mapping Services Department of The Automobile Association. (A03824)

A CIP Catalogue record for this book is available from the British Library.

Printed by Oriental Press in Dubai

Symbol	Description	Symbol	Description	Symbol	Description
Junction 9	Motorway & junction	County, administrative boundary	Theatre or performing arts centre, Cinema
Services	Motorway service area	Mounds		Golf course
	Primary road single/dual carriageway	City wall		Camping AA inspected
Services	Primary road service area	17 Page continuation 1:15,000		Caravan site AA inspected
	A road single/dual carriageway	3 Page continuation enlarged to 1:10,000		Camping & caravan site AA inspected
	B road single/dual carriageway	River/canal, lake, pier		Theme park
	Other road single/dual carriageway	Aqueduct, lock, weir		Abbey, cathedral or priory
	Minor/private road, access may be restricted	465 Winter Hill Peak (with height in metres)		Castle
	One-way street	Beach		Historic house or building
	Pedestrian area	Woodland	Wakehurst Place (NT)	National Trust property
	Track or footpath	Park		Museum or art gallery
	Road under construction	Cemetery		Roman antiquity
	Road tunnel	Built-up area		Ancient site, battlefield or monument
30	Speed camera site (fixed location) with speed limit in mph	Industrial/business building		Industrial interest
V	Speed camera site (fixed location) with variable speed limit	Leisure building		Garden
40 V	Section of road with two or more fixed camera sites; speed limit in mph or variable	Retail building		Garden Centre Garden Centre Association Member
50 → ← 50	Average speed (SPECS™) camera system with speed limit in mph	Other building		Garden Centre Wyevale Garden Centre
P P+	Parking, Park & Ride	A&E Hospital with 24-hour A&E department		Arboretum
	Bus/coach station	PO Post Office		Farm or animal centre
	Railway & main railway station	Public library		Zoological or wildlife collection
	Railway & minor railway station	Tourist Information Centre, Seasonal		Bird collection
	Light railway & station	Petrol station, 24 hour Major suppliers only		Nature reserve
	Preserved private railway	† Church/chapel		Aquarium
LC	Level crossing	Public toilet, with facilities for the less able	V Visitor or heritage centre
	Tramway	PH Public house AA recommended		Country park
	Ferry route	Restaurant AA inspected		Cave
	Airport runway	Madeira Hotel Hotel AA inspected		Windmill
					Distillery, brewery or vineyard

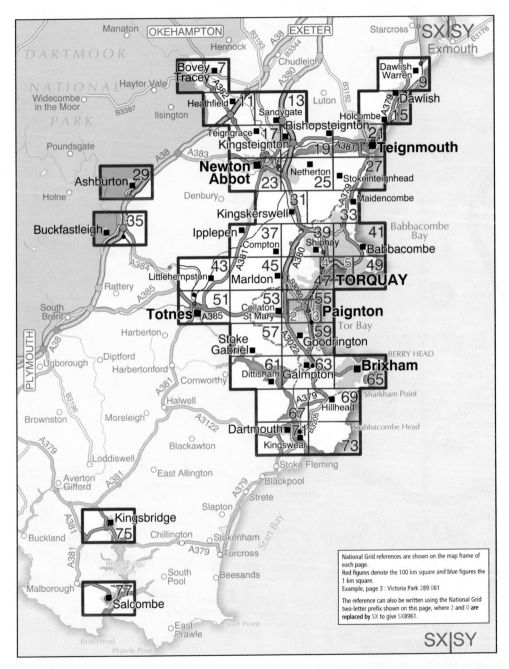

National Grid references are shown on the map frame of each page.
Red figures denote the 100 km square and blue figures the 1 km square.
Example, page 3 : Victoria Park 289 061

The reference can also be written using the National Grid two-letter prefix shown on this page, where 2 and 0 are replaced by SX to give SX8961.

Enlarged scale pages 1:10,000

6.3 inches to 1 mile

miles

kilometres

Scale of main map pages 1:15,000

4.2 inches to 1 mile

miles

kilometres

Brunel Business Centre

Colin Road

MARINE

Redcliffe Hotel

Marine Pk

H

55

J

K

Mead Cl
Mead La
Wilton Rd
Kings Road
Upr Mortn Tk

F

AD

G

S

89

90

Lower

Polsham

Oldenburg Pk

Road

Polsham Park

Victoria Park

ROAD

Steartfield Rd

Waterfield Rd
Norman Rd
Leighon Rd

1

19

ways
bing

Garfield Road

Esplanade

Paignton Pier

2

HYDE

ROAD

P

P

Victoria Shopping Centre

Beach Road

Berry Sq

Paignton Sands

Pksd Rd

Victoria Square

Kernou Road

ESPLANADE

Eastern

Esplanade

Apollo Cinema

LC

Victoria St

B3201

TORBAY ROAD

Queen's Pk Rd

Bowling Green

PAIGNTON

3

WESTERN

VICTORIA ST

P

P

Paignton Station
Paignton RFC & CC

Adelphi Road

B3201

P

RD

P

Adelphi Lane

Queens Rd

Stafford Rd

Queens Rd

Roundham Road

The Harbour

4

P

Queen's Park

LC

B3201

St Andrews Rd

Works

PO

Paignton Sailing & Rowing Club

Roundham Head

A379

WHITSTONE

ROAD

Hill Park Ter

W Orch

Cleveland Road

Keysfield Road

Belle Vue Road

Greylands Preparatory School

Vista Road

Cliff Road

Roundham Av

Roundham Head

5

The Riviera

Roundham Road

Summerhill Hotel

Young's Pk La

Braeside Road

Highcliffe Ms

Alta

Roundham Crs

Roundham Gardens

090

6

Great Western

Clennon Park

Young's Park Rd

Young's Park Road

Paignton & Dartmouth Steam Rlwy

Close

SW Coast Path Promenade

7

Tanners Road

89

90

F

G

Goodrington Station

H

59

J

K

or
eisure
entre

West Coast Path

Goodrington Sands

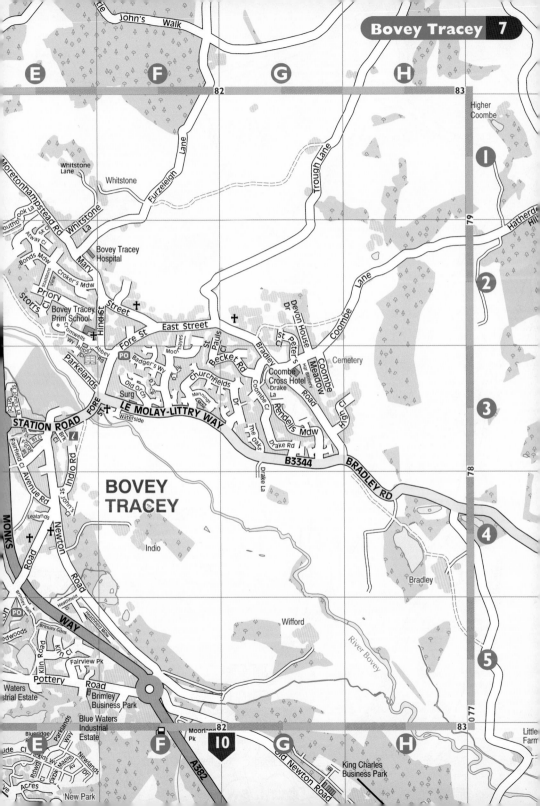

8

Port Road

A   B   C   Port Road   D

2 95   96

Hensford

Hensford Road

Branscombe Lane

Langdon Hospital

1

79

Long Lane

2

Ashcombe Road

Millcroft Farm

3

78

Langdon House

Long Lane

Langdon Farm

Langdon Road

Radfords

4

Lower Dawlish Water

Ford Gra

Gatehouse Farm

Gatehouse County Prim Sch

Sec

Elm Grove Road

5

077

Dawlish Water

Ashcombe Road

Long Lane

Badlake Hill

Badlake

The Humpy

Meadow Pk

Meadow Rise

Cavendish

Upper Longlands

Lanherne First Sch

Longlands

Summerland

The Paddock Hill

Gatehouse

Gatehouse Rise

Sutton Close

Newlands

Oak Park Rd

Oakwo Coll

Wallace Avenue

Old Gatehouse

East

Bere Hill

Empsons Hill

Weech Road

Stonelands Park

Vicarage Gardens

B

Ch St

Lwr Mdw

Old Town St

Stockton Hill

Stockton Rd

Regent St

15

Park Rd

Smld Cl

Stockton Av

King

Hosp

Health Cen

Priory Pk Rd

Orchard Cl

Priory Rd

High St

The Strand

Brook St

PO

Dawlish

C

D

2 95

96

1 grid square represents 500 metres

E F G H

Orchard Lane

97 98

Eastdon House

Dawlish Warren

Dawlish Warren National Nature Reserve

I

Shutterton Farm

Dawlish Warren

Shutterton Lane

Golf Course

79

Sherwell Cl

Warren Golf Club

Hazelwood Dr

Olive Gdns

S Av

Dawlish Warren Station

2

Poplar

Lakeside

Bracken Cl

P Cl

Olive Gv

Crs

Surgery

P

Shutterton Bridge

Sandpiper

Skylark

Cedar

Beechwood

Peppermint Park

Pine Tree Cl

East Devon Way

Beach Road

Golden Sands Holiday Park

Week Lane

Mount Pleasant Road

3

Warren Road

South West Coast Path

78

Langstone Cliff Hotel

Leadstone Camping

Little Week Road

4

Lower Higher Dr

Gilpin Cl

Carhaix Wy

Holman

Cl

Easter Rd

Drive

Dawlish Leisure Centre

Pinewood

Henty Cl

Henty AV

PO

Dawlish Town FC

A379

THE BROOKDOWE

EXETER ROAD

South West Coast Path

97 98

077

E F G H

DAWLISH

Knighton Heath
Nature Reserve

E   F   G   H

B3344

Pipehouse Lane

B3193

Little Bovey
Farm

atherines CE
ary School

Clay Lane

I

Jews Bridge

2

76

River Teign

hfield

Old Newton Road

Works

A38

brow Hill

Sharps Crest
Heath Hill
Sharps Crest

Heathfield
Cross

Brocks
Farm

3

12

Sharps Cl

Moorland
Gate

4

Stover
Country
Park

Stover Lake

Summer
Lane

A382

P

V

Leygreen

075

5

Newton Abbot
(Sto. Golf Club

E   F 16   G   H

Templer Way

Stover
School

Golf Course

Gappah

Gappah La

12

285 77

86

A B C D

Babcom

Bellamarsh
Barton

Gappah
Brake

1

B3193

2

76

John Acres Lane

Fosterville

River Te

3

II

075

4

Orchard
Close

5

Templer Way

Preston

LOWER PRESTON B3193

Sandygate

Clybrk Cl

Sandygate

Five La

285

86

A B 17 C D

Kingsteignton
Swimming Pool

Orchard
Meadow

Abbrook
Av

Avenue

Cross

Cemetery

Dr

Bus
Par

1 grid square represents 500 metres

Olchard

Olchard Lane

A380

Hamblecombe Lane

Town Farm Lane

Idef

E   F   G   H

88   89   77

I

Well Covert

2

76

Hestow Road

3

Combe

705

4

Whiteway
Barton

075

Hestow Road

5

Lindridge Hill   Lindridge Hill

Humber Lane

A380

Belmont

Ct

Rydon   Long

Barton

KINGSTEIGNTON 18

E   F   G   H

88   89

KINGSTEIGNTON

River Teign

E F G H

90 91

Ashwell

Cem

Higher Radway
Farm

Wolfsgrove

I

Bishopsteignton

Wood

Teignview Road

Manor Rd

Radway Gdns

Radwa

Grandison Cl

Wallis Gv

Bronescombe Av

Teignview Road

Great Furlong

Littlefield

Smith Hl

Berry Hl

Clanage St

Manor Dr

Tapley
Gardens

West
Street

Fore St

Shute Hl

Way Hl

74

2

Murley Cres

Murley
Grange

PO

Bishops
Ct

Bishops Avenue

Mitre Cl

Canons Cl

Deans Cl

Bishops Ct

Orcd

Road

Teign Cl

The Drive

Bishopsteignton
Primary School

Lawn's End

Moors Cl

Cockhaven Cl

The Hvn

Cockhaven
Manor
Hotel

C Mdl

St John's

†

Church Rd

3

Forder La

Horns
Pk

†

Cockhaven Cl

Stockmead Gardens

NEWTON ROAD

Newton Rd

A381

A381

NEWTON

Flow Lane

ROAD

Flow Lane

73

20

4

Coombe
Cellars

5

Templer Way

Netherton
House

072

E F G H

90 91

25

Shaldon Road

Park

Higher
Sackery

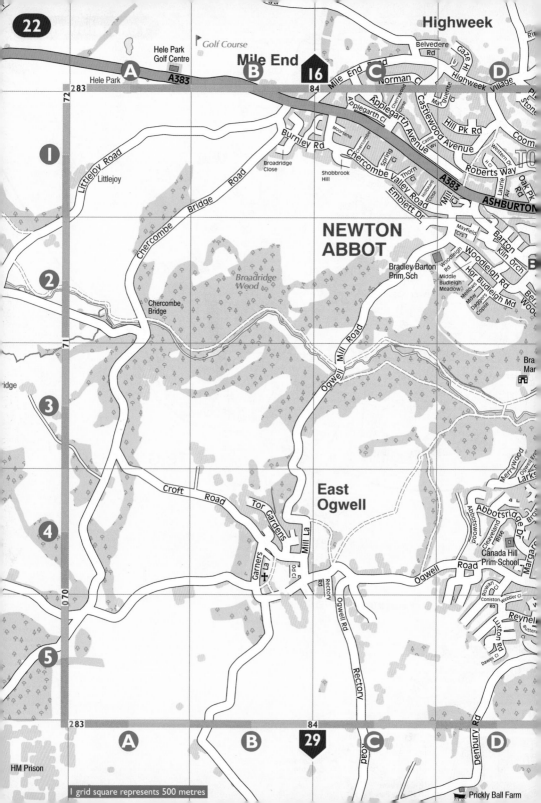

22

Highweek

Golf Course

Mile End

NEWTON
ABBOT

East
Ogwell

Hele Park
Golf Centre

Hele Park

A383

Littlejoy Road

Littlejoy

Chercombe Bridge Road

Broadridge
Close

Burnley Rd

Moorend

Shobbrook
Hill

Applegarth Cl

Applegarth Avenue

Chercombe Valley Road

Spring Cl

Thorn
Close

Horsham
Close

Emblett Dr

Belvedere
Rd

Gaze Hl

Norman C

Marguerite

Highweek Village

Hill Pk Rd

Castlewood Avenue

Castle
Wy

Roberts Way

Laurie
Av

Oak Pk
Rd

Coom

ASHBURTON

Mill

A383

Mayfield

Bradley Barton
Prim Sch

Woodleigh
Rd

Woodleigh Rd

Hgr Budleigh

Middle
Budleigh
Meadow

Mellows

Daggers
Copse

Mdw

Barton
Kiln Orch

Bel
Wood

Bra
Mar

Broadridge
Wood

Chercombe
Bridge

Ogwell Mill Road

Croft Road

Tor Gardens

Garners La

Mill La

Od Cl

Rectory
Rd

Rectory Road

Ogwell Rd

Ogwell Road

Canada Hill
Prim School

Merrywood

Larks

Abbotsridge Dr

Abbotswood

Cleaveland Rise

Margar

Ronan

Coniston
Rd

Webber Cl

Reynel
Cl

Luxton
Cl

Dawes Cl

Butterme

Denbury Rd

HM Prison

Prickly Ball Farm

1 grid square represents 500 metres

I

2

3

4

5

A B 16 C D

283

72

84

Mile End Rd

71

070

283

A B 29 C D

84

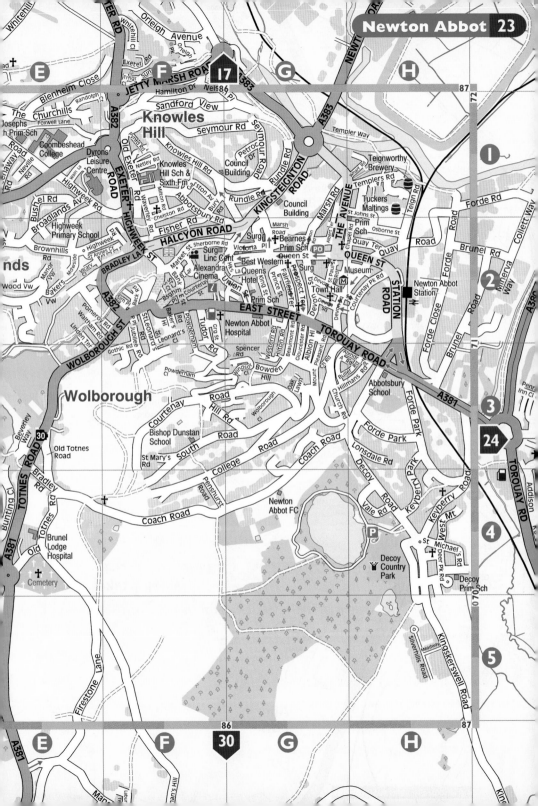

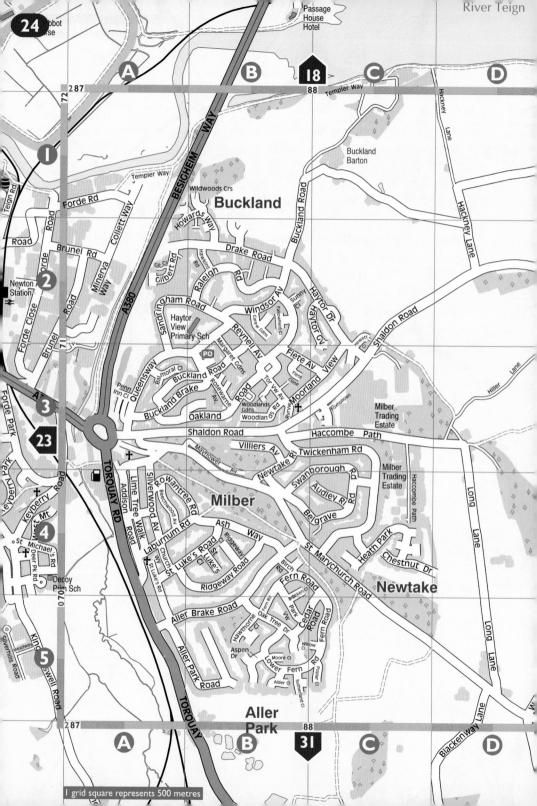

Coombe
Cellars

Templer Way

Netherton
House

E   F   **19**   G   H

90   72

Higher
Sackery

Cross Park

Shaldon Road

Combeinteignhead

† PH

Cross Hill

I

Mill Bottom Lane

2

71

Netherton

Charlecombe

Ridge Road

3

26

Haccombe

†

4

Haccombe
House

No Man's Land

070

5

E   F   **32**   G   H

90   91

Middle

Shaldon Prim.Sch

PO

Green

Strand

Fore St

Penrym

Pleasant La

Tree Gv

Middle street

Broadlands

Digmar St

Horse Lane

Marine

E

TORQUAY ROAD

F

Parade

21

G

H

94

95

72

The Ness House

Commons Old Rd

Picket Head Hill

Dunmore Dr

P

Ness Dr

Shaldon Wildlife Collection

Q14

Woodleigh Pk

Coast View Holiday Park

south west Coast Path

I

Lane

A379

Bundle Head

2

71

Commons

Labrador Bay

3

south west Coast Path

ROAD

4

070

5

94

95

E

F

G

H

A B C D

273 74

I

71

2

Ausewell
Wood

Amberley Cl
Old Mnr Cl

Headb

Hele

3

70

River Dart
Country Park

4

Knowle
Cl

5

Dartmoo
Lodge
Hotel

069

273 74

A B C D

Priestaford
House

I grid square represents 500 metres

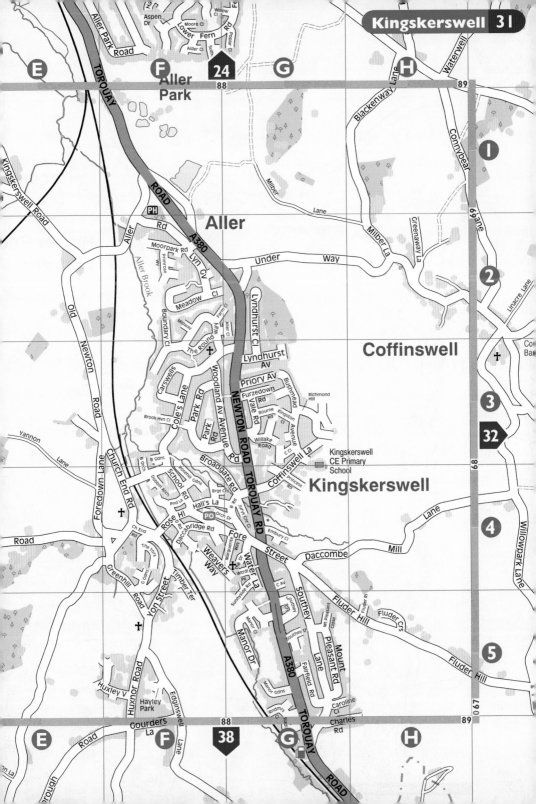

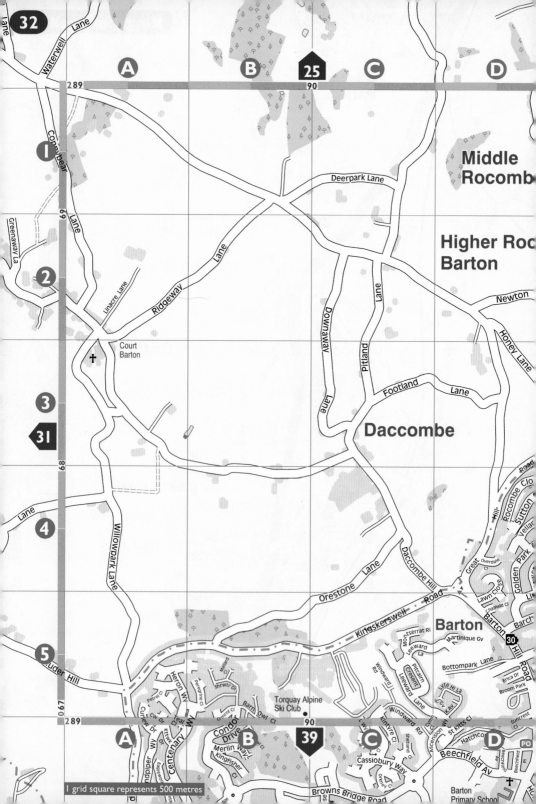

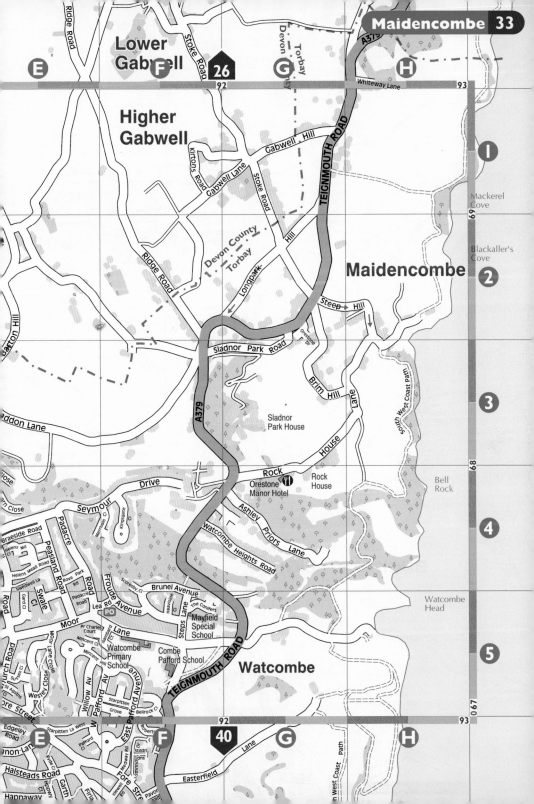

Ridge Road

Lower
Gabwell

Stoke Road

E **F** 26 **G** Torbay Devon **H**

92 Whiteway Lane 93

Higher
Gabwell

Kirtons Road

Gabwell Hill

Gabwell Lane

Stoke Road

TEIGNMOUTH ROAD

I

69

Mackerel Cove

Ridge Road

Devon County
Torbay

Longpark

Hill

Blackaller's
Cove

Maidencombe **2**

Steep Hill

Orestone Dr

Sladnor Park Road

Brim Hill

House Lane

South West Coast Path

3

68

A379

Sladdon Lane

Sladnor
Park House

Rock

Orestone
Manor Hotel

Rock
House

Bell
Rock

4

Drive

Seymour

Padacre

Close

Braeside Road

Peasland Road

Road

Swale Cl

Helens Mead

Kingsgate

Marivale Cl

Bove Park Rd

Padacre Road

Lea Rd

Scoresby Cl

Ashley Priors Lane

Watcombe Heights Road

The Conifers

Watcombe
Head

PO

Brunel Avenue

Froude Avenue

Moor

Pr Charles Court

Mincent Cl

Mincent Hill

Helensvale

Steps Lane

Mayfield
Special
School

5

067

Willow Av

W Pafford Av

Watcombe
Primary
School

Barnard Lane

Combe
Pafford School

TEIGNMOUTH ROAD

Watcombe

Church Road

St Agatha's

Wesley Cl

Mincent Close

Starpitten Grove

Bellrock Cl

Fore Street

East Pafford Avenue

Pafford Cl

Starpitten La West

Rye Cl

Steddh Dr

Medway Rd

Sidwell

Roberts

Lane

Easterfield Lane

Pavor

Edgeley
Road

non Lan

Halsteads Road

Garth

Hapnaway

E **F** 40 **G** **H**

92 93

South West Coast Path

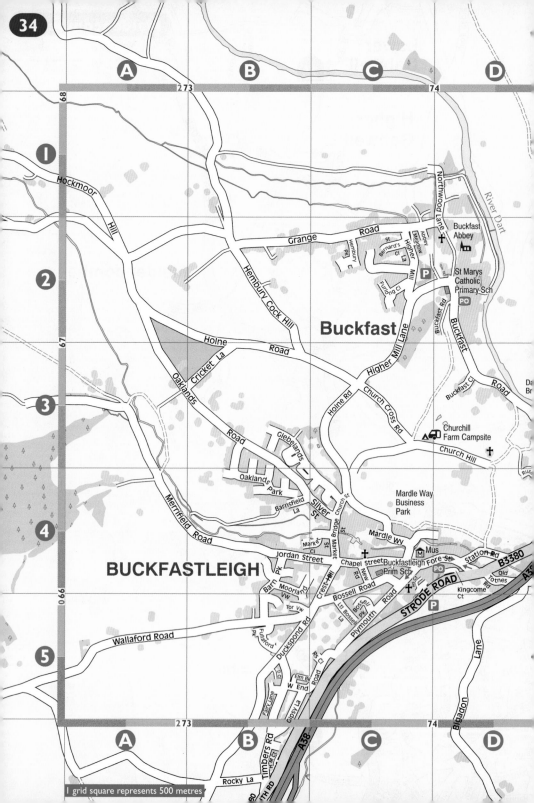

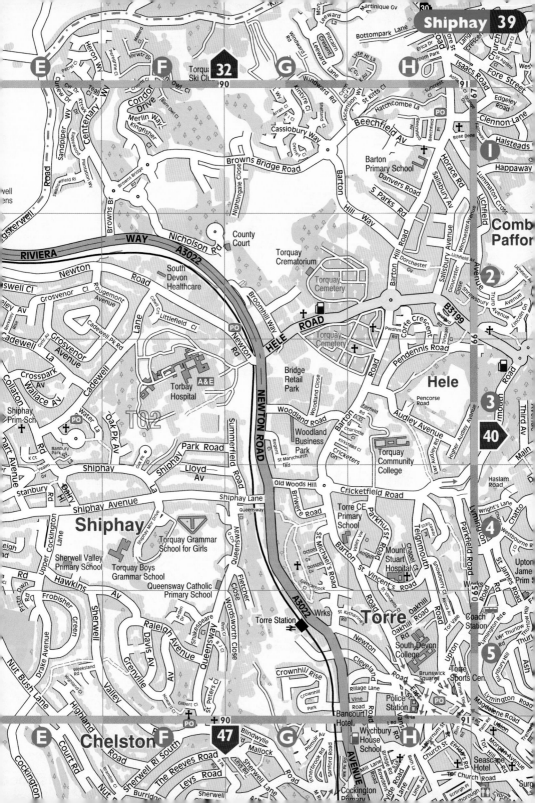

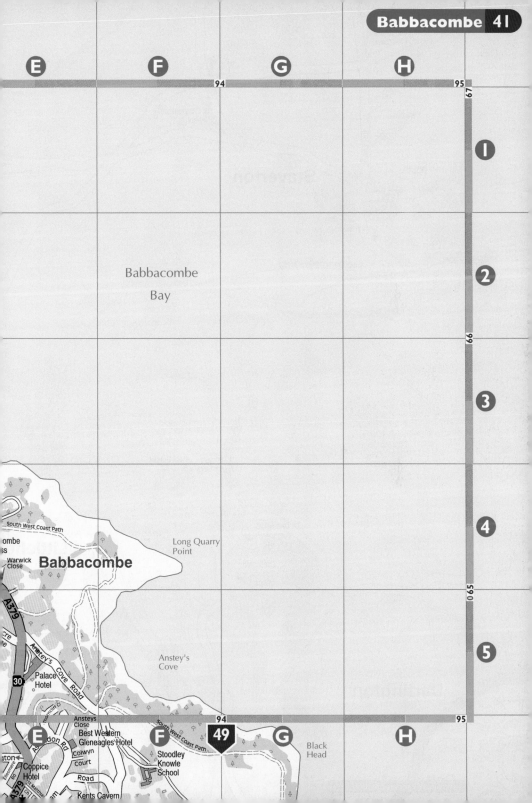

E   F   G   H

94   95

67

1

Babbacombe

Bay

2

66

3

South West Coast Path

ombe
ss

Warwick
Close

Babbacombe

Long Quarry
Point

4

065

A379

Anstey's
Cove Road

Anstey's
Cove

5

Palace
Hotel

30

Ansteys
Close

South West Coast Path

94   95

E   Best Western   F   **49**   G
Gleneagles Hotel

Black
Head

H

Coppice
Hotel

Colwyn
Court

Stoodley
Knowle
School

A379

Road

Kents Cavern

E F G H

82 83

Fishacre
Barton

Lillisford
Farm

Battleford Lane

I

64

Hemsford

Knaves
Ash Cross

PH

Tally House

Buckyette

Lane

2

Parsonage

A381

3

44

Uphempston

63

4

on

Lane

†

PH

A381

Coombe
Park

Gatcombe Brook

Netherton

5

62

er Hems

E F G H

82 83

51

44

A　　　**B**　　**36**　　**C**　　　**D**

2 83　　　　　　　　　　　　84

Combe House

Tanyard Lane

Footland
Lane

Waye
Barton

1

Battleford Lane

A381

64

Weekaborough

Woodhead Lane

Hernhi
Copse

2

3

A381

43

63

Loventor
Manor

4

Afton

tcombe Brook

5

Berry Pomoroy
Castle

062

2 83　　　　　　　　　　　　84

A　　　　**B**　　**52**　　**C**　　　　**D**

Berry
Castle Lodge

1 grid square represents 500 metres

E   F   **37**   G   H

86   87

I

2

Devon County
Torbay

Ipplepen Road

Aptor

Marldon   Lane   Ipplepen Road

La

oventor

Love Lane

Love Lane

Church Hill

PH

Village Road

Meadow Pk

Parkfield Cl

Millmans Rd

Peters Crs

Nether

Pye Pk

3

Vicarage Hill

46

Road

Marldon

Road

Kiln

Marldon Gv

Marldon CE
Primary School

Belfield
Belfield
Belfield

Way

Smallwell   Lane

Furzegood

Marldon Cross Hill

West Vw

Belfield Av

Five Lanes Rd

Vicarage Rd

Road

4

Wildwoods
Farm

Moorview

West
Vw Rd

PO

Chriscomb

Poplars Dr

Bampton Cl

Wixbrgh Dr

Churscombe Road

Farthing Lane

Totnes Road

Westerland Lane

Leader Lane

Brockhurst Park

Cntrn Cl

5

Westerland

Totnes Road

MARLDON WY

A380

Widend
Touring Park

Widdicombe Lane

County

Higher Ramshill Lane

Ho

46

A   B   38   C   D

287   88

I

Widdicombe
Farm

Widdicombe Farm
Touring Park

WAY

A380

Stantor Lane

64

HELLEVOETSLUIS

Stantor
Barton

2

Love Lane

Devon County Torbay

MARLDON - WY

Meadow L

Parkfield Cl

Pembroke Pk

Cockington   Road

's Crs   Rd

3

Nethe

Vicarage Hill

Occombe

Preston Down Road

Templer

Duchy Gardens

45

Belfield

Belfield

Preston Dn
Road

Road

Duchy
Pk

Duchy Avenue

Duchy

Beavers Brook

Deers Leap

Belfield AV

Vicarage Rd

63

Preston Down Road

Drive

Five Lanes Rd

Hill

Bampton Cl

Singmore Rd

TQ3

Sandringham

Lindsay Rd

Osborn Rd

Uplands Rd

Wilton Rd

Merriland Gdns

Marland Cl

Drive

4

combe Road

Leader Lane

Churscombe

Occombe   Valley

PO

5

A380

Windmll
La

Park

Green

Longmead

Road

Oketor

Road

Minn Tor

Tor

Kestor Dr

Greenfield

Cranford
Rd

Road

Alban

Cary
Rd

Lacy
Road

Windmill

AV

Windmill

Road

Road

Pres

062

Dolphin Court   Road

Dolphin Crs

Forest Rdg
Rd

Windmill
Road

Hutton
Road

Stella Rd

Gdns

Cecilia Rd

George
Road

287

James Av

Dixon
Cl

Dunstone Cl

Badger Cl

Shorton Rd

Alison   Rd

Graham Rd

Vale

Rhodanthe

Road

Road

Heights

Dunstone Park Rd

MARLDON

Mariners Way

Shorton

Barcombe

Sleepy

Southfield Aven

88

A   Pines   B   54   C   D Cecil

's Road   Rd   Barcombe   Road   Barcomb

PO   Maldenwa   Southfield   Winsu   Avenue   Surge

Ramshill   Road   Honeysuckles   Edenvale Rd   Southfield Avenue

amshill Lane

1 grid square represents 500 metres

Anstey's Cove

Palace Hotel

30

E **F** **41** **G** **H**

94 95

Ansteys Close

Best Western Gleneagles Hotel

Asheldon Rd

Thornbury Cl

Colwyn Court

Coppice Hotel

Stoodley Knowle School

A379

Road

Ilsham

Kents Cavern

Ilsham Close

South West Coast Path

Black Head

I

64

Ilsham CE Prim Sch

PO Kents Road

Ilsham Crescent

Ilsham

Ilsham Marine

Richmond Close

Lincombe

Lincombe Drive

Danby Hts Cl

Oxlea Road

Ridgeway Road

Meadfoot Cl

Bishops Close

Drive

Bishops Rise

Hope's Nose

2

Oxlea Close

The Woods

Ilsham Road

Whidborne Avenue

Avenue

South West Coast Path

Kilmorie

Kilmorie Close

Whidborne Cl

Thatcher

Thatcher Heights

Thatcher Av

Ilsham Marine Drive

3

63

Meadfoot Beach

Thatcher Rock

East Shag

4

5

62

94 95

E **F** **G** **H**

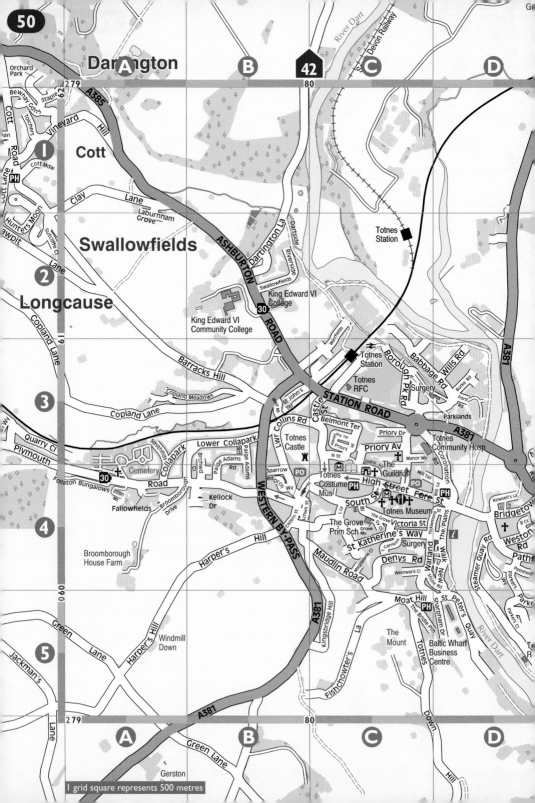

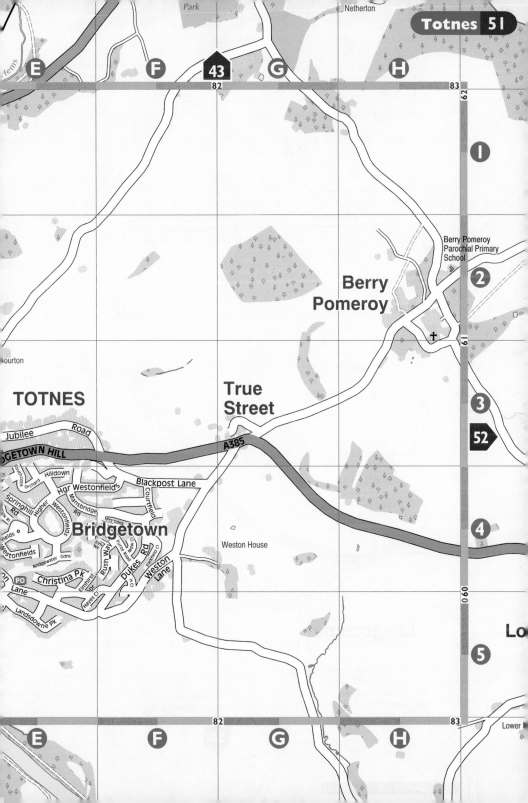

52

A · B · **44** · C · D

283
62

1

Berry Pomeroy
Castle

Berry
Castle Lodge

Berry Pomeroy
Parochial Primary
School

2

61

3

◀ **51**

Blagdon

Glazegate Lane

4

A385

TOTNES ROAD

060

Byslades
International
Touring &
Camping Park

Ayreville

5

Longcombe

283
84

Lower Longcombe

A · B · **56** · C · D

I grid square represents 500 metres

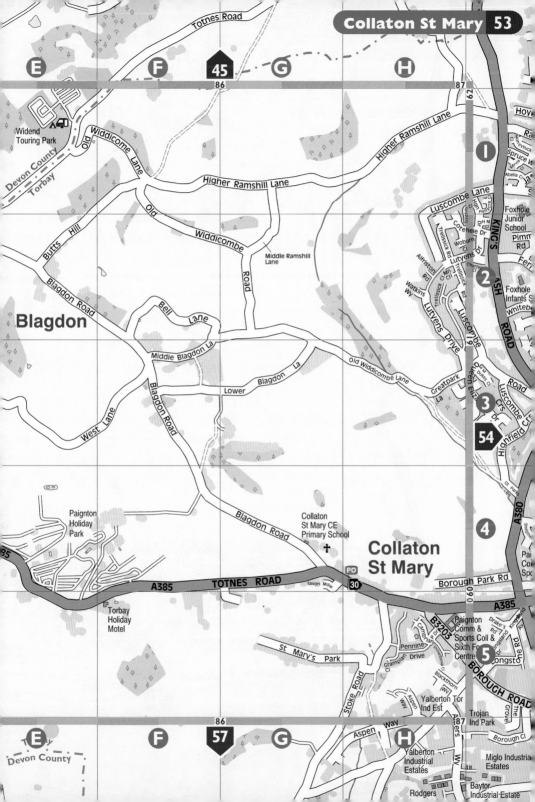

Hollicombe
Beach

Lower Penns Rd
Great Headland
Tarraway
A3022
St Paul's Rd
Forrescue Rd
Cedar Rd
Headland Road
Bay Vw
Malderek Av
Hd Cv
Locarno Av
Orient Road
Surg

E   **F**   47   90   **G**   **H**   91   62

on Rd
Butland
AV

POWcroft Rd
Old Torquay Road
PARIS RD
EUGENE RD
Morin Rd
Langs Rd
MANOR ROAD
orbay School
Upper Morin Rd
Colin Rd
Marine Pk
MARINE DRIVE
Prom
Marine Pde
Marine Gdns
The Rtrt
PO

I

Redcliffe
Hotel

2

Oldenburg Pk
Wakeford Rd
Steartfield Rd
Normor Rd
B3207
ESPLANADE ROAD
Esplanade
South West Coast Path
Paignton
Pier

Tor Bay

3

Garfield Road
Beach Road
Berry Sq
Kernou Road
Apollo
Cinema
Eastern
Adelphi Road
Adelphi La

PAIGNTON

61

NDS RD
Roundham
Works
Belle Vue
Cleveland Road
PO
Keysfield
Rd
Alta Vista Rd
Cliff Road
R Rd
Paignton Sailing
& Rowing Club
P
Roundham
Head

4

eylands
eparatory
hool
Roundham
Rd
Roundham
Crescent
Roundham Av
South W Coast Path
Summerhill Hotel
Roundham
Gdns

060

5

Promenade
3
E   ngton   **F**   59   90   **G**   **H**   91

Goodrington
Sands

Longcombe

A B **52** C D

283 84

Lower Longcombe

59

Fleet Mill

1

2

Aish

Aish Road

Holle Lane

3

58

Sharpham House

4

Holle La

Aish Road

Cro

Mapledene Cl

Orchard Wy

Palgn

The Yeolands

Pound Fld

Long

Barn Park

Flood St

Stoke Gabriel

River Dart

Vicarage Road

Millers La

Maddicks Orch

Hayes Cl

Paignton

New Road

Duncannon

5

Sha m Wood

Duncannon Lane

School Hill

Darton Cv

Duncannon Mill

Stoke Gabriel Primary School

Mill Hill

Mill Hill

Barnway

Shu

57

283 84

A B **60** C D

Stoke

Woods

Long st

E F `53` G H

Motel

St Mary's Park

Comm & Sports Coll &

203

BOROUGH ROAD

Blackthorn

Yalberton Tor Ind Est

Trojan Ind Park

Borough Cl

Aspen Way

Yalberton Industrial Estates

Miglo Industria Estates

Torbay Devon County

I

Bay Industrial Estate

Rodgers Industrial Estate

Yalberton Road

Works

Sup

59

TQ

Aish Road

Yalberton

Lwr Yalberton Road

2

Broadleigh Farm Park

Whitehill

Whitehill Country Park

Long Road

Lane

Long

3

Stoke Road

Whitehill

`58`

Road

Paignton Road

Whitehill Lane

Higher Well Farm Holiday Park

58

Port Bridge

Torbay Devon Count

4

Path

Broad

Lane

Lower Well Farm

5

Mill

Byter

Waddeton Road

57

`86` `87`

E F `61` G H

South Downs

E   F   55   G   H

90   91

Goodrington
Station

Goodrington
Sands

I

Cliff Pk
Av

Cliff Park Road   Sthn Sands
Wk
Oyster Cl

The Saddle

59

PO

Barn Rd

2

Seafields   Crossway

Horseshoe
Bend

Saltern
Cove

30

Saltern
Road

Red Brook Cl

stone

3

Waterside Rd

Broadsands

58

The Cl

Broadsands
Pk Rd

Blue Waters Drive

Paignton & Dartmouth Steam Railway

Broadsands
Bend

4

Av

Broadsands

Broad
Reach

P

Elberry Lane

South West Coast Path

5

Elberry
Farm

Sycamore
Cl

Elberry
Cove

Long Wools

South West Coast Path

Broadsands

Road

Brunel   Road   90   Elberry   91   0 57

Bracken
Rd

E   F   63   G   H

Bascombe   Road

Fowden

Stone
Park

Warborough

Kennels
Rd

▲ *Golf Course*

E F **57** G H

86 87

57

1

Waddeton Road

Byter

Mill

South Downs

Sandridge

Pighole Point

2

56

Dart

Lower Gurrow Point

3 Rive

Blackness Rock

62

Riverside Road

4

Dittisham

Dittisham Court

nworthy

Lower St

Higher Street

Ham Lane

P

The Level

The Lane

The Quay

P

Manor St

PH

Passenger Ferry

Greenway

Gree Gard

5

0 55

Cott Farm

Bozom-eal Cross

86 66 87

E F **66** G H

62

A   B   **58**   C   D

57   287   88

Waddeton

1

Waddeton
Court

Stoke

Road

Galmpton

Langdon Fields

Higher Warborough

Langdon Lane

Dart View Rd

Stoke

Hillrise

Gabriel

The Roundings

Road

2

56

Galmpton Creek

Manor
Farm

The
Orchards

PO

The
Coombe

Old   Road

Galmpton Farm Cl

**Galmpton
CE Primary
School**

Greenway

River Dart

Lower
Gurrow
Point

3

61

Light
La

**Galmpton
Touring Park**

Greenway Rd

055

Mill   Lane

Mill La

4

Lower
Greenway

Paignton & Dartmouth Steam Railway

Greenway   Road

Combe

Greenway   Road

**Passenger
Ferry**

5

Greenway
Garden (NT)

Maypool

Higher
Greenway

287

88

A   B   **67**   C   D

I grid square represents 500 metres

Broadsands

Broad Beach

E

P

Elberry Farm

F

Broadsands Road

Sycamore

Elberry Lan

South West Coast Path

59

90

G

Elberry Cove

Elberry

South West Coast Path

H

91

57

Brunel Road

Lower Fowden Road

Wools

Stone Park

Bracken Rl

Warborough Rd

Brakeridge Cl

Bascombe Road

DARTMOUTH

Manor Bend

Churston Golf Club

Fairway Close

Bascombe Road

Camellia Close

Bridge Road

Kennels Rd

Elberry Lane

Golf Course

I

Links Cl

Green Lane

✝

2

Norr

sanders Rd

Pom

PK

Copythorne

Swather Wy

Lavender Cl

Way Road

Churston Close

Churston Station

Churston Ferrers Grammar School

Bascombe Road

Churston Ferrer's Gn

Copythorne

Wayside

Wayside

Hortfield Cl

3

64

A3022

ROAD

Barn Court

Churston Road

Churston Ferrers

TQ5

Alston Farm

Alston Lane

NEW R

Laywell Rd

4

KENNELS ROAD

A379

Lupton House

Coniston Cl

55

Deep Dene

Summercourt

5

Alston La

Lupton Park

Summercourt Wy

Huccaby Cl

Huccaby Cl

Believer

Bala Brook

Yew Cl

Chestnut

Tor Drive

Packhall

Chestnut Prim Sch

Rowan Way

Elizabeth Av

Ocean View

E

F

68

90

G

H

91

Guzzle Down

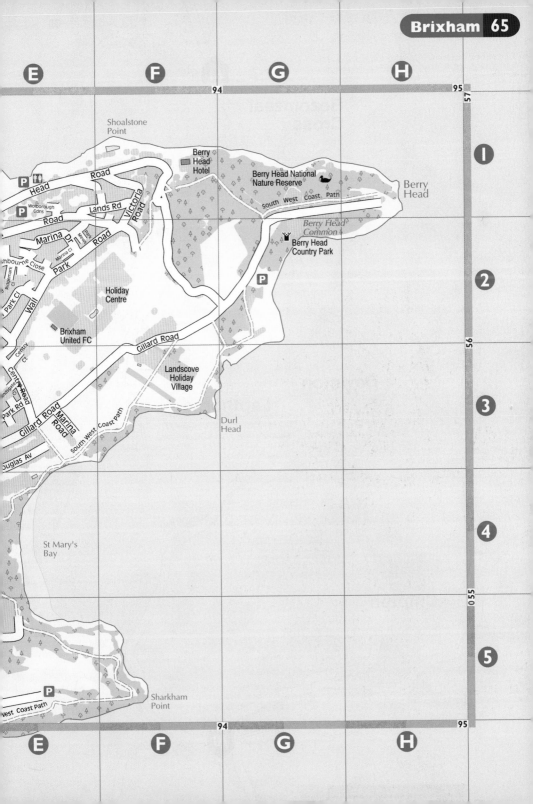

E   F   G   H

94   95   57

I

Shoalstone
Point

Berry
Head
Hotel

Berry Head National
Nature Reserve

Berry
Head

P   🚻   Head   Road

South   West   Coast   Path

Wolborough
Cdns

P   Road   Lands Rd   Victoria   Road

*Berry Head
Common*

2

Marina   Park   Road   Berry Head
Country Park

hbourne Close

Marina Cl

P

Park Cl

Ridgemark Cl

Wall

Holiday
Centre

56

Brixham
United FC

Centry
Ct

Gillard Road

Landscove
Holiday
Village

3

Park Rd

Centry Road

Durl
Head

Gillard Road

Marina
Road

South West Coast Path

Ouglas Av

055

4

St Mary's
Bay

5

P

West   Coast Path

Sharkham
Point

E   F   G   H

94   95

Greenway Garden (NT)

Maypool

Higher Greenway

62

E   F   G   H

88   89

I

54

2

River Dart

Long Wood

Paignton & Dartmouth Steam Railway

BRID

A379

3

68

53

Higher Noss Point

4

Hoodown Farm

Rough Hole Point

BRIDGE ROAD

B3205

A379

5

052

LC

The Dart Marina Hotel

The Esplanade

Road   The Backs

Naida V

Britannia RN College

Sandquay Rd

Vehicle Ferry

89

Queen Elizabeth Av

Beat TV

Way

Flagstaff

Road

Prince of Wales of the Coombe

COOMBE RD

N EMBNKMNT

88

mouth Amateur Club

71

E   F   G   H

Cemetery

Commanders Cut

A379

Dartmouth Harbour

Waterhead Brake

HIGHER CO

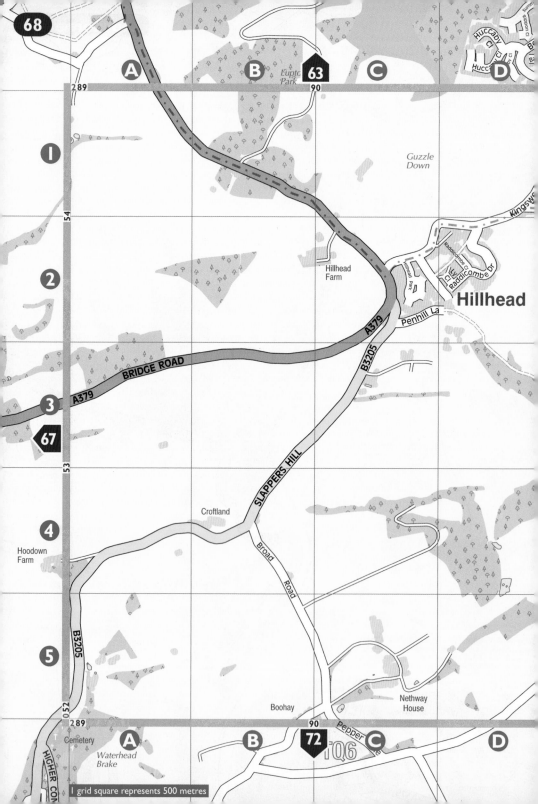

68

A   B   63   C   D

289

54

1

Guzzle
Down

2

Hillhead
Farm

Kingswe

Raddicombe Cl
Raddicombe Dr

Hillhead

A379

Penhill La

BRIDGE ROAD

B3205

A379

3

67

53

SLAPPERS HILL

Croftland

4

Hoodown
Farm

Broad Road

B3205

5

52

Boohay

Nethway
House

289

Cemetery

Pepper

A   B   72   C   D

Waterhead
Brake

HIGHER CO

TQ6

1 grid square represents 500 metres

Chestnut
Elm Rd
Tor Cl
Maple
Drive
Cedar
Milton
Cl
Golden Cl
Upton Hl Rd
Yards Lane

Maple
Road
Milton Street
Quentin Av
Chiseldon Hill
Folafield
springdale Cl
Yards Lane

Milton PK
Milton Crs
Southdown
Nut Tree Orch
Chiseldon Farm

E   **F**   **64**   **G**   **H**

Milton Flds
92
South West Coast Path
93

Ocean View Dr

Challeycroft Road   Yards Lane   Torbay   **I**
Devon County   54

Mill   Southdown Road   Southdown Cliff

Lane   Southdown Farm   **2**

Mansands   South West Coast Path

Lane   Man
Sands   **3**

Woodhuish Lane   Crabrock
Point   53

P

ish Farm   **4**

Long
Sands

South West Coast Path

Scabbacombe Lane   **5**

P   0 52

92   **73**   93
E   **F**   **G**   **H**
Sc...mbe
Sa...

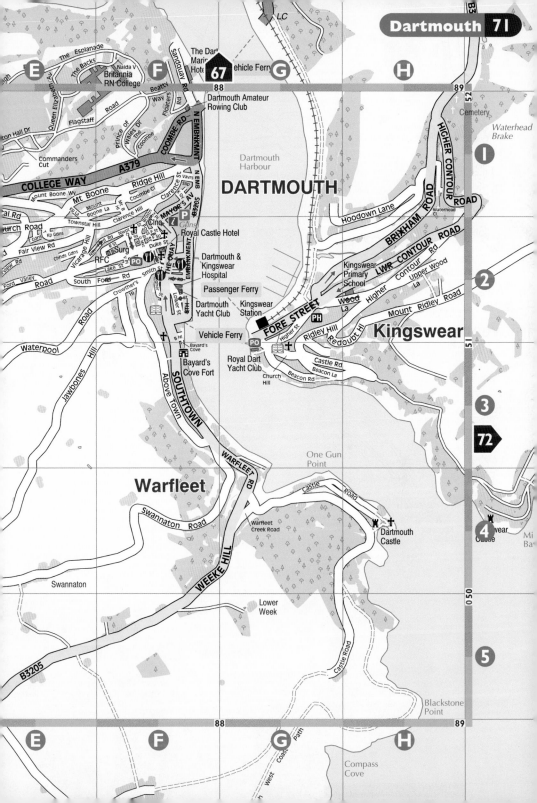

E F G H

The Esplanade
The Backs
Naida V
Britannia
RN College
Beatty
Floaters
Way
Sandquay Rd
Prince of Wales Dr
Commanders Cut
Flagstaff
Queen Elizabeth Av
Coombe
COOMBE RD.
N EMBANKMNT
The Dart
Mari
Hote
ehicle Ferry
67
Dartmouth Amateur
Rowing Club
Dartmouth Harbour
89
52
Cemetery
Waterhead Brake
I

Hall Dr
A379
COLLEGE WAY
Mount Boone Wy
Mt. Boone
Ridge Hill
Coombe Hill
Mount Boone La
Clarence Hill
Townstal Hill
Vavrs
N EMB
Slip
Clarence St
Coombe Cl
Mayor's Av
B3205
DARTMOUTH
Hoodown Lane
HIGHER CONTOUR ROAD
BRIXHAM ROAD
Waterhead Cl

Rd
Ch Rd
Fair View Rd
Vicarage Hill
Chfrds Gdns
Kp Gdns
Clng
Royal Castle Hotel
Gdns
i
P
LWR CONTOUR ROAD
Higher Contour Rd
Upper Wood La
2
51

Surg
RFC
PO
Lake St
Smith St
HW RD
Dartmouth & Kingswear Hospital
Kingswear Primary School
Wood La
Mount Ridley Road
Kingswear

Ford Valley Road
South Ford Rd
Crowther's
Duke St
THE QUAY
N EMBANKMNT
Collier St
Higher St
STH
Passenger Ferry
Dartmouth Yacht Club
Kingswear Station
FORE STREET
Wood
Higher
Ridley Hill
Redoubt Hl
PH

Waterpool Road
Jawbones Hill
SOUTHTOWN
Above Town
B Hi
B Hi
Vehicle Ferry
PO
Bayard's Cove
Bayard's Cove Fort
Royal Dart Yacht Club
Church Hill
Castle Rd.
Beacon La
Beacon Rd

Warfleet
Swannaton Road
WARFLEET RD
WEEKE HILL
Warfleet Creek Road
One Gun Point
Castle Road
Dartmouth Castle
wear
ale
Mi
Ba
50
4
72
3

Swannaton
Lower Week
Blackstone Point
050
5

E F G H
88
89
West Coast Path
Compass Cove

72

B3205

A

B

Boohay

68

C

Nethway
House

D

52 289

90

Cemetery

Waterhead
Brake

Pepper Lane

TQ6

HIGH

1

CONTOUR ROAD

Kingston

XHAM ROAD

CONTOUR ROAD

Waterhead

Mount Ridley Road

Contour Rd La

Upper Wood
La

2

ount Ridley Road

Coleton Farm

gswear

5

P

3

Higher
Brownstone
Farm

71

mouth
e

4

Kingswear
Castle

Warren
House

Mill
Bay Cove

050

5

South West Coast Path

Newfoundland
Cove

Outer Fro
Point

Blackstone
Point

Inner
Froward Point

M
St

289

90

A

B

C

D

1 grid square represents 500 metres

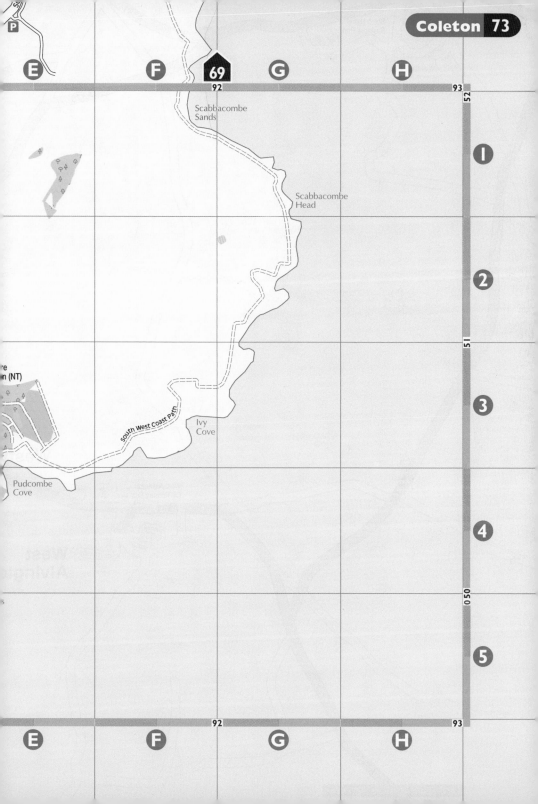

E F **69** G H

92 93 **52**

Scabbacombe
Sands

1

Scabbacombe
Head

2

51

re
n (NT)

3

South West Coast Path Ivy
Cove

Pudcombe
Cove

4

050

5

92 93

E F G H

PO
Scott's Cl
Clebeland
Woodlar
South Hams
Business Park

A   **B**   **C**   **D**   Da

A381

271   72   A379

45

1

A381

2

Brownringsleigh
Wood

3

West Alvington
Wood

West

44

4

A381

West Alvington
CE Primary Sch

A381

Townsend Rd
Townsend Cl
LWR ST

Wood Rd

Town Park

WEST

WEST

Kingsbr
College

West
Alvingto

Longfields

5

043

271   72

A   **B**   **C**   **D**

A381

1 grid square represents 500 metres

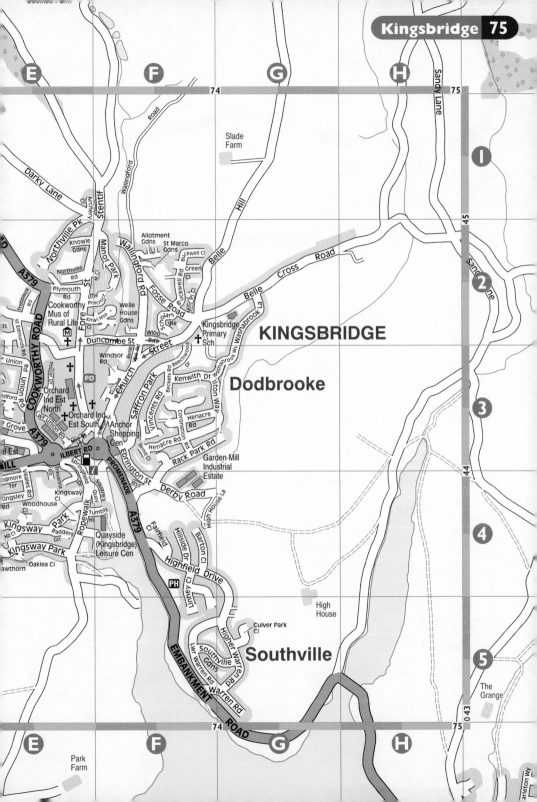

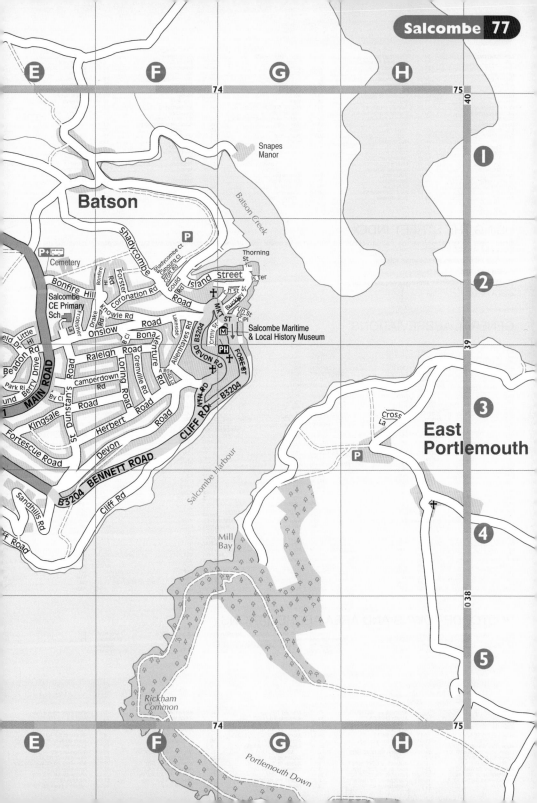

E F G H

74 75 40

I

Snapes Manor

Batson Batson Creek

2

39

P Shadycombe Thorning St

Cemetery Shadycombe ct St Ter

Capburn Cl Coff Rd

Bonfire Hill Forster Rd Gould Island Street

Bonfire Rd Un St St

Salcombe Coronation Rd MKT ST Buckley Un St

CE Primary Knowle Rd Road C Pl

Sch Drake Cl Lakeside M Salcombe Maritime

Onslow Road & Local History Museum

Frobisher Bona B3204 PH

Little Raleigh Road Adventure Rd DEVON RD FOREST

Beadon Rd Camperdown Loring Road Grenville Rd Allenhayes Rd

Park Ri Berry Drive Rd

By Cl St Dunstan's INFIRMARY RD Cross

und Kingsale Road Herbert Road CLIFF RD B3204 La East

MAIN ROAD Road Devon Portlemouth

Fortescue Road BENNETT ROAD 3

B3204 Cliff Rd P

Sandhills Rd Salcombe Harbour 38

f Road Cliff Rd

Mill Bay 4

Rickham Common

5

Portlemouth Down

E F G H

74 75

USING THE STREET INDEX

Street names are listed alphabetically. Each street name is followed by its postal town or area locality, the Postcode District, the page number, and the reference to the square in which the name is found.

Standard index entries are shown as follows:

Abbey Cl *BVYTR* TQ13 ....**7** E3

Street names and selected addresses not shown on the map due to scale restrictions are shown in the index with an asterisk:

Albert Pl *TOT* TQ9 * **50** C4

GENERAL ABBREVIATIONS

ACC	ACCESS	CTS	COURTS	HGR	HIGHER	MTN	MOUNTAIN	RP
ALY	ALLEY	CTYD	COURTYARD	HL	HILL	MTS	MOUNTAINS	RW
AP	APPROACH	CUTT	CUTTINGS	HLS	HILLS	MUS	MUSEUM	S	S
AR	ARCADE	CV	COVE	HO	HOUSE	MWY	MOTORWAY	SE	SC
ASS	ASSOCIATION	CYN	CANYON	HOL	HOLLOW	N	NORTH	SER	SERVICE
AV	AVENUE	DEPT	DEPARTMENT	HOSP	HOSPITAL	NE	NORTH EAST	SH
BCH	BEACH	DL	DALE	HRB	HARBOUR	NW	NORTH WEST	SHOP	SHO
BLDS	BUILDINGS	DM	DAM	HTH	HEATH	O/P	OVERPASS	SKWY	SK
BND	BEND	DR	DRIVE	HTS	HEIGHTS	OFF	OFFICE	SMT	SU
BNK	BANK	DRO	DROVE	HVN	HAVEN	ORCH	ORCHARD	SOC	SC
BR	BRIDGE	DRY	DRIVEWAY	HWY	HIGHWAY	OV	OVAL	SP
BRK	BROOK	DWGS	DWELLINGS	IMP	IMPERIAL	PAL	PALACE	SPR	S
BTM	BOTTOM	E	EAST	IN	INLET	PAS	PASSAGE	SQ	SC
BUS	BUSINESS	EMB	EMBANKMENT	IND EST	INDUSTRIAL ESTATE	PAV	PAVILION	ST	ST
BVD	BOULEVARD	EMBY	EMBASSY	INF	INFIRMARY	PDE	PARADE	STN	ST
BY	BYPASS	ESP	ESPLANADE	INFO	INFORMATION	PH	PUBLIC HOUSE	STR	ST
CATH	CATHEDRAL	EST	ESTATE	INT	INTERCHANGE	PK	PARK	STRD	ST
CEM	CEMETERY	EX	EXCHANGE	IS	ISLAND	PKWY	PARKWAY	SW	SOUTH
CEN	CENTRE	EXPY	EXPRESSWAY	JCT	JUNCTION	PL	PLACE	SWY	TRA
CFT	CROFT	EXT	EXTENSION	JTY	JETTY	PLN	PLAIN	TDG	TR
CH	CHURCH	F/O	FLYOVER	KG	KING	PLNS	PLAINS	TER	TEF
CHA	CHASE	FC	FOOTBALL CLUB	KNL	KNOLL	PLZ	PLAZA	THWY	THROUG
CHYD	CHURCHYARD	FK	FORK	L	LAKE	POL	POLICE STATION	TNL	TL
CIR	CIRCLE	FLD	FIELD	LA	LANE	PR	PRINCE	TOLL	TO
CIRC	CIRCUS	FLDS	FIELDS	LDG	LODGE	PREC	PRECINCT	TPK	TURI
CL	CLOSE	FLS	FALLS	LGT	LIGHT	PREP	PREPARATORY	TR
CLFS	CLIFFS	FM	FARM	LK	LOCK	PRIM	PRIMARY	TRL
CMP	CAMP	FT	FORT	LKS	LAKES	PROM	PROMENADE	TWR	T
CNR	CORNER	FTS	FLATS	LNDG	LANDING	PRS	PRINCESS	U/P	UNDER
CO	COUNTY	FWY	FREEWAY	LTL	LITTLE	PRT	PORT	UNI	UNIVE
COLL	COLLEGE	FY	FERRY	LWR	LOWER	PT	POINT	UPR	UPR
COM	COMMON	GA	GATE	MAG	MAGISTRATES'	PTH	PATH	V	V
COMM	COMMISSION	GAL	GALLERY	MAN	MANSIONS	PZ	PIAZZA	VA	V
CON	CONVENT	GDN	GARDEN	MD	MEAD	QD	QUADRANT	VIAD	VIA
COT	COTTAGE	GDNS	GARDENS	MDW	MEADOWS	QU	QUEEN	VIL
COTS	COTTAGES	GLD	GLADE	MEM	MEMORIAL	QY	QUAY	VIS	VIS
CP	CAPE	GLN	GLEN	MI	MILL	R	RIVER	VLG	VII
CPS	COPSE	GN	GREEN	MKT	MARKET	RBT	ROUNDABOUT	VLS	VLS
CR	CREEK	GND	GROUND	MKTS	MARKETS	RD	ROAD	VW	V
CREM	CREMATORIUM	GRA	GRANGE	ML	MALL	RDG	RIDGE	W	W
CRS	CRESCENT	GRG	GARAGE	MNR	MANOR	REP	REPUBLIC	WD	W
CSWY	CAUSEWAY	GT	GREAT	MS	MEWS	RES	RESERVOIR	WHF	W
CT	COURT	GTWY	GATEWAY	MSN	MISSION	RFC	RUGBY FOOTBALL CLUB	WKS	W
CTRL	CENTRAL	GV	GROVE	MT	MOUNT	RI	RISE	

POSTCODE TOWNS AND AREA ABBREVIATIONS

BRIX	Brixham	DAW	Dawlish	NWTAB	Newton Abbot	SPH/CHEL/BTN	Shiphay/	TOT	To
BUCKF	Buckfastleigh	GDRG/BDS	Goodrington/	PAIGN	Paignton		Chelston/	TQ	To
BVYTR	Bovey Tracey		Broadsands	REXSW	Rural Exeter south & west		Barton		
DART	Dartmouth	KING	Kingsbridge	SALC	Salcombe	TEIGN	Teignmouth		

A

		Abbrook Av *NWTAB* TQ12	17 H1	Aish Rd *TOT* TQ9	56 C2	Alexandra La *TQ* TQ1	5 H1	Aller Park Rd *NWTAB* TQ12
		Abelia Cl *PAIGN* TQ3	54 A1	Alandale Rd *TEIGN* TQ14	21 G2	Alexandra Rd *NWTAB* TQ12	23 G3	Aller Rd *NWTAB* TQ12
		Above Town *DART* TQ6	71 F3	Albany Rd *PAIGN* TQ3	46 C5	*TO* TQ1	40 B5	All Hallows Rd *PAIGN* TQ3
		Acacia Cl *NWTAB* TQ12	18 B5	Albert Pl *TOT* TQ9 *	50 C4	Alexandra Ter *NWTAB* TQ12	23 G3	Allotment Gdns *KING* TQ7
Abbey Cl *BVYTR* TQ13	7 E3	Acadia Rd *TQ* TQ1	49 E2	Albert Rd *TQ* TQ1	5 G2	*SPH/CHEL/BTN* TQ2 *	4 C1	All Saints Rd *TQ* TQ1
TEIGN TQ14	21 G1	Acland Rd *SALC* TQ8	77 F3	Albert St *DAW* EX7	15 F1	*TEIGN* TQ14	21 F4	Alma Rd *BRIX* TQ5
Abbey Crs *SPH/CHEL/BTN* TQ2	5 F2	Acre La *TQ* TQ1	41 E5	Albert Ter *BVYTR* TQ13 *	7 E3	*TOT* TQ9	50 C5	Alpine Rd *TQ* TQ1
Abbey Meadow *BUCKF* TQ11	34 C2	Addison Rd *GDRG/BDS* TQ4	2 C5	*NWTAB* TQ12	23 G2	Alfriston Rd *PAIGN* TQ3	53 H2	Alston La *BRIX* TQ5
Abbey Rd *BVYTR* TQ13	7 E3	*NWTAB* TQ12	24 A4	Albion Hl *NWTAB* TQ12	23 G3	Alison Rd *PAIGN* TQ3	46 C5	Alta Vista Cl *TEIGN* TQ14
SPH/CHEL/BTN TQ2	5 F1	Adelphi La *GDRG/BDS* TQ4	3 G4	Albion St *TEIGN* TQ14	21 E5	Allenhayes La *SALC* TQ8	77 F3	Alta Vista Rd *GDRG/BDS* TQ4
Abbotsbury Rd *NWTAB* TQ12	23 F1	Adelphi Rd *GDRG/BDS* TQ4	3 G3	Alder Cl *NWTAB* TQ12	24 B5	Allenhayes Rd *SALC* TQ8	77 F3	Amberley Cl *BVYTR* TQ13
Abbotsridge Dr *NWTAB* TQ12	18 D2	Admirals Wk *TEIGN* TQ14	14 A5	Alder Cl *NWTAB* TQ12		Aller Brake Rd *NWTAB* TQ12	24 A5	Andor Av *NWTAB* TQ12
Abbotswood *NWTAB* TQ12	18 B2	Ailescombe Dr *PAIGN* TQ3	2 B2	*TEIGN* TQ14		Aller Cl *NWTAB* TQ12	31 G2	Ansteys Cl *TQ* TQ1
NWTAB TQ12	22 D4	Ailescombe Rd *PAIGN* TQ3	2 B2	Alders Wy *GDRG/BDS* TQ4	53 H5	Aller Hl *DAW* EX7	14 D2	Anstey's Cove Rd *TQ* TQ1
				Alexander Rd *DAW* EX7	15 F1	Aller Hl *DAW* EX7		

ea Rd PAIGN TQ3 46 B5
: St DART TQ6 71 F2
garth Av NWTAB TQ12 22 C1
garth Cl NWTAB TQ12 22 C1
rcade
H/CHEL/BTN TQ2 * 5 H4
ry Cl KING TQ7 75 E1
St TEIGN TQ14 21 E5
vay Dr DART TQ6 70 D1
Dr SPH/CHEL/BTN TQ2 39 F5
da Dr TEIGN TQ14 14 A5
Cl SPH/CHEL/BTN TQ2 39 G1
gton TQ TQ1 39 H4
sion Wy
H/CHEL/BTN TQ2 39 H1
rn Wk GDRG/BDS TQ4 58 D4
rton Rd BVYTR TQ13 7 E5
TAB TQ12 22 D1
T TQ9 50 B2
mbe Rd DAW EX7 8 A5
don Rd TQ TQ1 49 E1
eld Rd
H/CHEL/BTN TQ2 4 A2
ill Rd TQ TQ1 40 A5
TEIGN TQ14 20 A2
gh Cl
H/CHEL/BTN TQ2 32 D5
GN TQ14 21 F1
gh Ct TQ TQ1 48 D3
gh Dr TEIGN TQ14 21 F1
gh Mt TEIGN TQ14 21 F1
gh Pk TEIGN TQ14 21 F1
gh Ri TEIGN TQ14 21 F1
gh Rd KING TQ7 74 D4
gh Wy TEIGN TQ14 21 F1
Priors La TQ TQ1 33 G4
Wy DAW EX7 8 D5
d NWTAB TQ12 18 A4
n Ct NWTAB TQ12 13 E5
n Ter TQ TQ1 49 E1
y NWTAB TQ12 24 B4
Dr NWTAB TQ12 24 B5
Wy GDRG/BDS TQ4 57 H1
Cl BVYTR TQ13 7 E2
y Av SPH/CHEL/BTN TQ2 39 H3
y Ri NWTAB TQ12 24 C4
nd Rd TQ TQ1 40 C4
e Rd BVYTR TQ13 7 E4
TAB TQ12 31 F3
H/CHEL/BTN TQ2 4 C1
venue NWTAB TQ12 23 G2
Hl NWTAB TQ12 18 A2
Av TQ TQ1 39 H5
Rd SPH/CHEL/BTN TQ2 38 D4

B

combe Downs Rd
TQ1 40 C3
combe Rd TQ TQ1 48 D2
age Rd TOT TQ9 50 C3
Rd NWTAB TQ12 23 F2
acks DART TQ6 67 E5
er Cl DART TQ6 70 D1
GN TQ3 46 B5
ers Cl KING TQ7 74 D4
TAB TQ12 17 H2
ers Gn KING TQ7 75 E4
er's Wy BVYTR TQ13 7 F3
ke Cl DAW EX7 15 E1
ke Hl DAW EX7 8 B5
s Hl BRIX TQ5 64 C4
's Hl NWTAB TQ12 23 F2
s Vw NWTAB TQ12 23 E2
rook Cl BRIX TQ5 63 H5
ill Rd KING TQ7 74 D4
d La BVYTR TQ13 29 C2
oral Cl NWTAB TQ12 24 A3
fylde Rd
H/CHEL/BTN TQ2 4 C2
ton Cl PAIGN TQ3 45 H4
ury Pk
H/CHEL/BTN TQ2 39 E3
La BRIX TQ5 64 C2
St NWTAB TQ12 23 F2
GN TQ14 21 G4
ington Av
H/CHEL/BTN TQ2 32 D5
mbe Hts PAIGN TQ3 54 C1
mbe La PAIGN TQ3 54 D1
mbe Rd PAIGN TQ3 54 C1
vell Cl TQ TQ1 40 B3
vell Rd TQ TQ1 40 B3
Ct BRIX TQ5 63 G2
ield Cl BRIX TQ5 62 D2
ield Rd BRIX TQ5 64 D4
GN TQ3 2 C1
H/CHEL/BTN TQ2 47 F4
arnhay TOT TQ9 56 D5
ill Rd NWTAB TQ12 31 G4
owl Cl
H/CHEL/BTN TQ2 32 B5
Pk BUCKF TQ11 34 B4
TAB TQ12 10 B5
T TQ9 56 D4
Park Cl NWTAB TQ12 36 C1
ark Cl TEIGN TQ14 21 G2
ark Rd TEIGN TQ14 21 G3
ark Ter TEIGN TQ14 21 G2
Rd GDRG/BDS TQ4 59 E2
Cl NWTAB TQ12 18 A4
field La BUCKF TQ11 34 B4
ey Cl TEIGN TQ14 21 G3
ley Dr TEIGN TQ14 21 G3
cks Hl TOT TQ9 50 A3
don Cl
H/CHEL/BTN TQ2 32 D4
gton Rd TQ TQ1 49 E1
n Av PAIGN TQ3 2 A2
n Cl KING TQ7 75 F4
GN TQ3 54 B2
n Crs DAW EX7 15 E1
GN TQ3 2 A1
n Dr NWTAB TQ12 22 D2
n Gdns PAIGN TQ3 2 A1
n Hl DAW EX7 15 F1
TQ1 33 E3

Barton Hill Rd
SPH/CHEL/BTN TQ2 39 H2
Barton Hill Wy
SPH/CHEL/BTN TQ2 39 G1
Barton La DAW EX7 15 E1
TOT TQ9 42 A1
Barton Rd PAIGN TQ3 2 A1
TQ TQ1 39 G4
Barum Cl PAIGN TQ3 3 G1
Bascombe Cl BRIX TQ5 63 F1
Bascombe Rd BRIX TQ5 63 E1
Bath La SPH/CHEL/BTN TQ2 4 C2
Bath Ter TEIGN TQ14 21 G4
Batson Gdns GDRG/BDS TQ4 2 D6
Battersway Rd
GDRG/BDS TQ4 54 A5
Battleford La TOT TQ9 43 H1
Battle Rd NWTAB TQ12 10 D3
Bayard's Cove DART TQ6 71 F3
Bayards Cove Steps
DART TQ6 * 71 F2
Bayard's Hl DART TQ6 71 F2
Baymount PAIGN TQ3 2 D1
Bay Vw PAIGN TQ3 47 F5
Bay View Dr TEIGN TQ14 21 G2
Bay View Steps BRIX TQ5 * 64 D2
Bay Vw West BRIX TQ5 * 64 C2
Beach Rd DAW EX7 9 G2
GDRG/BDS TQ4 3 G2
TQ TQ1 40 D3
Beach St DAW EX7 15 G1
Beach Wk GDRG/BDS TQ4 59 E2
Beacon Hl TQ TQ1 5 H6
Beacon La DART TQ6 71 G3
Beacon Rd DART TQ6 71 G3
Beacon Ter TQ TQ1 5 H6
Beadon Dr SALC TQ8 76 D3
Beadon Rd SALC TQ8 76 D4
Beanhay Cl NWTAB TQ12 10 B5
Bearne's La NWTAB TQ12 23 F2
Beatty Wy DART TQ6 71 F1
Beaumont Cl NWTAB TQ12 10 A5
SPH/CHEL/BTN TQ2 39 F5
Beaumont Rd NWTAB TQ12 23 G3
Beavers Brook Cl PAIGN TQ3 46 D4
Becket Rd BVYTR TQ13 7 F3
Beckets Rd KING TQ7 75 F3
Bedford Rd TQ TQ1 40 D3
Beechdown Pk
GDRG/BDS TQ4 * 53 F5
Beech Dr NWTAB TQ12 36 C1
Beechfield Av
SPH/CHEL/BTN TQ2 39 H1
Beechfield Pl
SPH/CHEL/BTN TQ2 39 H1
Beechwood Av NWTAB TQ12 24 A4
Beechwood Ct TEIGN TQ14 20 D1
Beechwood Crs DAW EX7 9 F2
Beechwood Dr KING TQ7 75 F3
Beenland Pl
SPH/CHEL/BTN TQ2 * 39 H5
Belfield Av PAIGN TQ3 45 H4
Belfield Cl PAIGN TQ3 45 H3
Belfield Ri PAIGN TQ3 45 H3
Belfield Rd PAIGN TQ3 54 A2
Belfield Wy PAIGN TQ3 45 H3
Belgrave Rd NWTAB TQ12 24 B4
SPH/CHEL/BTN TQ2 4 D3
Belgrave Ter TEIGN TQ14 21 G3
Belgravia Ter DART TQ6 * 71 G2
Bella Vista Rd BRIX TQ5 64 C1
Belle Cross Rd KING TQ7 75 G2
Belle Hl KING TQ7 75 F2
Bellever Tor Dr BRIX TQ5 63 H5
Belle Vue BRIX TQ5 * 64 C3
Belle Vue Rd GDRG/BDS TQ4 3 G5
KING TQ7 75 F3
Bell La PAIGN TQ3 53 F2
Bellrock Cl SPH/CHEL/BTN TQ2 33 F5
Belmont Cl NWTAB TQ12 18 A1
Belmont Rd BRIX TQ5 64 B3
TQ TQ1 40 C5
Belmont Ter TOT TQ9 50 C3
Belvedere Rd NWTAB TQ12 16 C5
Bench Tor Cl
SPH/CHEL/BTN TQ2 38 D3
Benedict Cl TEIGN TQ14 21 G1
Benedicts Cl NWTAB TQ12 10 B5
Benedicts Rd NWTAB TQ12 10 B5
Ben Jonson Cl
SPH/CHEL/BTN TQ2 39 F5
Benlears Acre NWTAB TQ12 10 B5
Bennett Rd SALC TQ8 77 E4
Ben Venue Cl TQ TQ1 5 J2
Berachah Rd TQ TQ1 40 B5
Berea Rd TQ TQ1 40 C5
Bere Hl DAW EX7 14 D1
Berkeley Av
SPH/CHEL/BTN TQ2 39 E2
Berkeley Ri
SPH/CHEL/BTN TQ2 39 E2
Berretts Wy NWTAB TQ12 10 C5
Berry Av PAIGN TQ3 2 B2
Berry Cl NWTAB TQ12 30 B2
SALC TQ8 77 E3
Berry Dr PAIGN TQ3 2 B2
Berry Head Rd BRIX TQ5 65 E2
Berry Hl TEIGN TQ14 19 H2
Berry La NWTAB TQ12 18 A4
Berry Meadow NWTAB TQ12 18 A4
Berry Rd PAIGN TQ3 2 B3
Berry Sq GDRG/BDS TQ4 3 G2
Berrys Wd NWTAB TQ12 22 D2
Besigheim Pl NWTAB TQ12 23 F2
Besigheim Wy NWTAB TQ12 24 A1
Bethel Ter TQ TQ1 5 H1
Beverley Ri BRIX TQ5 64 B3
Beverley Wy NWTAB TQ12 23 E3
Bexley La SPH/CHEL/BTN TQ2 4 C1
Bickford La TEIGN TQ14 21 G4
Bickfords Gn NWTAB TQ12 10 B5
Bickley Rd NWTAB TQ12 37 G1
Bidwell Brook Dr
GDRG/BDS TQ4 58 D3
Bigbury Wy
SPH/CHEL/BTN TQ2 40 B1
Biltor Rd NWTAB TQ12 36 B2
Bingfield Cl TQ TQ1 5 J2
Birch Rd NWTAB TQ12 24 B4
Birchwood Cl TOT TQ9 50 B4

Bishops Av TEIGN TQ14 19 H2
Bishops Cl TQ TQ1 49 F2
Bishops Ct TEIGN TQ14 19 H2
Bishop's Pl PAIGN TQ3 2 E3
Bishops Ri TQ TQ1 49 G2
Bishopsteignton Rd
TEIGN TQ14 20 D4
Bishop Wilfrid Rd TEIGN TQ14 20 D2
Bitney La NWTAB TQ12 30 C3
Bitton Av TEIGN TQ14 21 F3
Bitton Ct TEIGN TQ14 21 E3
Bitton Park Rd TEIGN TQ14 21 E3
Blackball La BRIX TQ5 64 C1
Blackberry Wy NWTAB TQ12 18 A1
Blackbrook Av GDRG/BDS TQ4 58 D4
Blackenway La NWTAB TQ12 31 H1
Blackhaven Cl GDRG/BDS TQ4 58 D4
Blackpost La TOT TQ9 51 F4
Blackstone Rd NWTAB TQ12 36 B2
Blackthorn Wy
GDRG/BDS TQ4 53 H5
Blagdon Rd PAIGN TQ3 52 D2
Blake Cl TQ TQ1 40 B3
Blatchcombe Dr PAIGN TQ3 54 B2
Blatchcombe Rd PAIGN TQ3 54 B2
Blenheim Cl NWTAB TQ12 23 E1
TQ TQ1 49 E2
Bligh Cl TEIGN TQ14 14 A5
Blindwell Av NWTAB TQ12 18 A3
Blindwylle Rd
SPH/CHEL/BTN TQ2 4 A1
Blueball Hl TOT TQ9 50 C4
Blueridge Rd BVYTR TQ13 10 A1
Blue Waters Dr
GDRG/BDS TQ4 59 E4
Blythwoods Crs TQ TQ1 40 B4
Body Hayes Cl TOT TQ9 56 C5
Bolton St BRIX TQ5 64 C3
Bonair Cl BRIX TQ5 64 C4
Bonaventure Cl SALC TQ8 77 F3
Bonaventure Rd SALC TQ8 77 F2
Bonds Meadow BVYTR TQ13 7 E2
Bonfire Hl SALC TQ8 77 F2
Borough Cl GDRG/BDS TQ4 58 A1
Borough Park Rd PAIGN TQ3 54 A4
TOT TQ9 50 C3
Borough Rd GDRG/BDS TQ4 54 A5
TQ TQ1 40 B2
Borthay Orch NWTAB TQ12 * 30 B1
Boscawen Pl TEIGN TQ14 21 F3
Bossell Pk BUCKF TQ11 34 C5
Bossell Rd BUCKF TQ11 34 C5
Bottompark La
SPH/CHEL/BTN TQ2 32 D5
Boundary Cl NWTAB TQ12 31 F2
Boundary Rd
SPH/CHEL/BTN TQ2 47 F1
Bourne Ct BRIX TQ5 63 H5
Bourne Rd NWTAB TQ12 31 G3
Bourton La TOT TQ9 51 E3
Bourton Rd TOT TQ9 51 E3
Bove Park Rd
SPH/CHEL/BTN TQ2 33 E4
Bovey Tracey Rd NWTAB TQ12 16 D4
Bowden Hl BVYTR TQ13 28 D4
NWTAB TQ12 23 G3
Bowden Rd NWTAB TQ12 36 B1
Bowdens Cl BVYTR TQ13 7 E3
Bowerland Av
SPH/CHEL/BTN TQ2 32 D4
Bowland Cl GDRG/BDS TQ4 58 B2
Boyds Dr TEIGN TQ14 21 G3
Bracken Cl NWTAB TQ12 24 B5
Bracken Ri GDRG/BDS TQ4 63 E1
Bracken Wy DAW EX7 9 F2
Bradden Crs BRIX TQ5 64 B3
Braddons Cliffe TQ TQ1 * 5 H3
Braddons Hill Rd East TQ TQ1 5 H3
Braddons Hill Rd West TQ TQ1 5 H4
Bradley La NWTAB TQ12 23 F2
Bradley Park Rd TQ TQ1 40 B2
Bradley Rd BVYTR TQ13 7 G2
NWTAB TQ12 23 E4
Braeside Ms GDRG/BDS TQ4 * 3 G6
Braeside Rd GDRG/BDS TQ4 3 G6
SPH/CHEL/BTN TQ2 33 E4
Brakeridge Cl BRIX TQ5 63 E1
Bramble Cl
SPH/CHEL/BTN TQ2 47 E1
Branksome Cl PAIGN TQ3 47 E4
Branscombe Cl TQ TQ1 40 D5
Branscombe La DAW EX7 8 B1
Brantwood Cl GDRG/BDS TQ4 2 C7
Brantwood Crs
GDRG/BDS TQ4 58 C1
Brantwood Dr GDRG/BDS TQ4 58 C1
Breakneck Hl TEIGN TQ14 14 B5
Brendons Av
SPH/CHEL/BTN TQ2 47 E3
Brent Rd PAIGN TQ3 2 E2
Briary La TQ TQ1 5 G1
Bridge Rd BRIX TQ5 63 F2
DART TQ6 67 G4
SPH/CHEL/BTN TQ2 4 C1
TEIGN TQ14 21 E5
Bridge St BUCKF TQ11 34 C4
KING TQ7 75 F3
NWTAB TQ12 36 B1
Bridgetown TOT TQ9 50 D4
Bridgetown Ct TOT TQ9 50 D4
Bridgetown Hl TOT TQ9 51 E4
Bridgewater Gdns TOT TQ9 51 E4
Bridle Cl GDRG/BDS TQ4 58 D4
Brim Hl TQ TQ1 33 G3
Brimlands BRIX TQ5 64 B3
Brimley Dr TEIGN TQ14 21 G3
Brimley Gdns BVYTR TQ13 7 E5
Brimley Halt BVYTR TQ13 7 E4
Brimley La BVYTR TQ13 6 C5
Brimley Rd BVYTR TQ13 6 D5
Brimley V BVYTR TQ13 6 D4
Briseham Cl BRIX TQ5 64 D4
Briseham Quarry BRIX TQ5 * 64 D5
Briseham Rd BRIX TQ5 64 D4
Britannia Av DART TQ6 70 C2
Briwere Rd
SPH/CHEL/BTN TQ2 39 G4
Brixham Rd DART TQ6 71 H2
GDRG/BDS TQ4 58 A2
Broadacre Dr BRIX TQ5 64 D2

Broadgate Crs NWTAB TQ12 31 F4
Broadgate Rd NWTAB TQ12 31 F3
Broadlands TEIGN TQ14 21 E5
Broadlands Av NWTAB TQ12 23 E1
Broadlands Rd GDRG/BDS TQ4 2 D6
Broadley Dr
SPH/CHEL/BTN TQ2 47 E3
Broadmeadow La TEIGN TQ14 20 D3
Broadmeadow Vw
TEIGN TQ14 20 D3
Broadpark BVYTR TQ13 6 D5
Broad Pk DART TQ6 70 D2
Broadpark Rd PAIGN TQ3 54 B1
SPH/CHEL/BTN TQ2 47 E4
Broad Pth TOT TQ9 57 E5
Broad Reach GDRG/BDS TQ4 59 E5
Broadridge Cl NWTAB TQ12 22 B1
Broad Rd DART TQ6 68 B4
Broadsands Av
GDRG/BDS TQ4 59 E5
Broadsands Bend
GDRG/BDS TQ4 59 E4
Broadsands Ct GDRG/BDS TQ4 58 D5
Broadsands Park Rd
GDRG/BDS TQ4 59 E4
Broadsands Rd
GDRG/BDS TQ4 63 E1
Broad Steps BRIX TQ5 * 64 D2
Broadstone DART TQ6 71 F2
Broadstone Park Rd
SPH/CHEL/BTN TQ2 47 F3
Broadway Av NWTAB TQ12 17 H2
Broadway Rd NWTAB TQ12 17 G3
Brockhurst Pk PAIGN TQ3 45 H4
Bronescombe Av TEIGN TQ14 20 A2
Bronshill Ms TQ TQ1 40 B5
Bronshill Rd TQ TQ1 40 B5
Brook Cl BVYTR TQ13 7 E3
DAW EX7 15 E5
Brookdale Cl BRIX TQ5 64 B3
Brookdale Pk BRIX TQ5 64 B3
Brookedor Gdns NWTAB TQ12 31 F3
Brookfield Cl NWTAB TQ12 18 A3
PAIGN TQ3 55 E1
Brookfield Dr TEIGN TQ14 21 G1
Brook Haven Cl NWTAB TQ12 31 F3
Brooklands TOT TQ9 50 D4
Brooklands La
SPH/CHEL/BTN TQ2 4 A4
Brook La TEIGN TQ14 20 D5
Brook Orch NWTAB TQ12 31 F3
Brook Rd NWTAB TQ12 36 B1
Brookside KING TQ7 75 E4
Brookside Cl TEIGN TQ14 21 E3
Brook St DAW EX7 15 F1
Brookvale Orch TEIGN TQ14 26 D1
Brook Wy NWTAB TQ12 12 D5
Broomborough Dr TOT TQ9 50 A4
Broom Cl DAW EX7 9 E4
Broomhill Wy
SPH/CHEL/BTN TQ2 39 G2
Broom Pk SPH/CHEL/BTN TQ2 32 D5
Brow Hl NWTAB TQ12 11 E3
Brownhills Rd NWTAB TQ12 23 E2
Brownings Wk NWTAB TQ12 22 D4
Browns Bridge Rd
SPH/CHEL/BTN TQ2 39 F1
Brunel Av SPH/CHEL/BTN TQ2 33 F4
Brunel Cl TEIGN TQ14 21 G2
Brunel Rd GDRG/BDS TQ4 63 F1
NWTAB TQ12 23 H3
Brunswick Pl DAW EX7 15 G1
Brunswick Sq
SPH/CHEL/BTN TQ2 39 H5
Brunswick St TEIGN TQ14 21 G4
Brunswick Ter TQ TQ1 39 H5
Buckeridge Av TEIGN TQ14 21 F2
Buckeridge Rd TEIGN TQ14 21 F2
Buckfast Cl BUCKF TQ11 34 D3
Buckfast Rd BUCKF TQ11 34 D2
Buckland Brake NWTAB TQ12 24 A3
Buckland Rd NWTAB TQ12 24 A3
Buckley St SALC TQ8 77 G2
Buckwell Cl KING TQ7 75 F2
Buckwell Rd KING TQ7 75 F2
Budleigh Cl TQ TQ1 40 D5
Buller Rd NWTAB TQ12 23 G3
Bunting Cl NWTAB TQ12 23 E4
TEIGN TQ14 21 E2
Burch Gdns DAW EX7 8 D3
Burke Rd TOT TQ9 50 D3
Burleigh Rd
SPH/CHEL/BTN TQ2 39 E4
Burnham Ct NWTAB TQ12 18 A3
Burnley Rd NWTAB TQ12 22 B1
Burn River Ri
SPH/CHEL/BTN TQ2 38 D3
Burnthouse Hl NWTAB TQ12 38 A2
Burridge Av
SPH/CHEL/BTN TQ2 47 F1
Burridge La
SPH/CHEL/BTN TQ2 5 F2
Burridge Rd
SPH/CHEL/BTN TQ2 4 A2
Burton Pl BRIX TQ5 64 C3
Burton St BRIX TQ5 64 C4
Burton Vil BRIX TQ5 64 C3
Burton Villa Cl BRIX TQ5 64 C3
Bury Rd NWTAB TQ12 23 F1
Bushel Rd NWTAB TQ12 23 E2
Bushmead Av NWTAB TQ12 31 G3
Butland Av PAIGN TQ3 47 E5
Butland Rd NWTAB TQ12 17 H2
Buttercombe Cl NWTAB TQ12 22 D5
Butterfly La TEIGN TQ14 26 C2
Butts Hl PAIGN TQ3 53 E2
Byron Rd TQ TQ1 40 A3
Byter Mill La TOT TQ9 57 E5

C

Cabbage Hl BVYTR TQ13 29 E5
Cabourg Cl SALC TQ8 77 F2
Cadewell Crs
SPH/CHEL/BTN TQ2 39 F2
Cadewell La
SPH/CHEL/BTN TQ2 39 E3
Cadewell Park Rd
SPH/CHEL/BTN TQ2 39 E2
Cadwell Rd PAIGN TQ3 2 E1
Calvados Pk NWTAB TQ12 18 B3
Camborne Crs GDRG/BDS TQ4 58 D4
Cambrian Cl GDRG/BDS TQ4 53 H5
Cambridge Rd BRIX TQ5 64 A3
TQ TQ1 40 B2
Camden Rd TQ TQ1 5 H1
Camellia Cl BRIX TQ5 63 F1
Camperdown Rd SALC TQ8 77 E3
Cannon Rd NWTAB TQ12 11 E3
Canons Cl TEIGN TQ14 19 H2
Captains Rd NWTAB TQ12 17 H2
Carew Gdns NWTAB TQ12 24 B2
Carey Rd DART TQ6 70 C2
Carhaix Wy DAW EX7 9 E4
Carlile Rd BRIX TQ5 64 A2
Carlton Cl PAIGN TQ3 47 E4
Carlton Dr PAIGN TQ3 47 E4
Carlton Ms TQ TQ1 * 40 C5
Carlton Pl TEIGN TQ14 21 G4
Carlton Rd TQ TQ1 40 C5
Caroline Cl NWTAB TQ12 31 G5
The Carrions TOT TQ9 50 C4
Carswells NWTAB TQ12 31 F3
Cartwright Crs TEIGN TQ14 20 D2
Cary Av TQ TQ1 40 C4
Cary Pde SPH/CHEL/BTN TQ2 5 H4
Cary Pk TQ TQ1 40 B4
Cary Park Rd TQ TQ1 40 C4
Cary Rd PAIGN TQ3 46 C5
SPH/CHEL/BTN TQ2 5 F3
Cassiobury Wy
SPH/CHEL/BTN TQ2 39 G1
Castle Chambers TQ TQ1 * 4 E1
Castle Circ SPH/CHEL/BTN TQ2 5 F1
Castle Gdns TQ TQ1 * 5 F1
Castle La PAIGN TQ3 37 G5
TQ TQ1 5 G1
Castle Rd DART TQ6 71 G5
TQ TQ1 5 G1
Castle St TOT TQ9 50 C3
Castle Wy NWTAB TQ12 22 C1
Castlewood Av NWTAB TQ12 22 C1
Castor Cl BRIX TQ5 64 C4
Castor Rd BRIX TQ5 64 C5
Catherine Crs GDRG/BDS TQ4 2 B6
Caunters Cl NWTAB TQ12 36 B1
Causeway NWTAB TQ12 * 36 B1
Cavalier Rd NWTAB TQ12 10 D2
Cavalry Dr NWTAB TQ12 10 D4
Cavendish Cl DAW EX7 8 B5
Cavern Rd BRIX TQ5 64 C3
TQ TQ1 5 H1
Cayman Cl SPH/CHEL/BTN TQ2 39 G1
Cecil Av PAIGN TQ3 54 D1
Cecilia Rd PAIGN TQ3 46 C5
Cecil Ms PAIGN TQ3 2 E2
Cecil Rd PAIGN TQ3 2 E1
Cedar DAW EX7 9 F2
Cedar Cl TEIGN TQ14 21 H1
Cedar Court Rd TQ TQ1 40 B4
Cedar Rd NWTAB TQ12 24 B5
PAIGN TQ3 47 E5
Cedars Rd TQ TQ1 48 D1
The Cedars TOT TQ9 * 51 E3
Cedar Wy BRIX TQ5 64 A5
Centenary Wy
SPH/CHEL/BTN TQ2 39 E1
Central Av PAIGN TQ3 2 E1
Centry Ct BRIX TQ5 65 E3
Centry Rd BRIX TQ5 65 E3
Chalfield Cl
SPH/CHEL/BTN TQ2 32 D5
Challabrook La BVYTR TQ13 6 D4
Challeycroft Rd BRIX TQ5 69 E1
Chantry Cl TEIGN TQ14 21 H1
Chapel Ct TQ TQ1 39 H4
Chapel La TOT TQ9 50 D4
Chapel Pl BVYTR TQ13 * 7 F2
Chapel Rd NWTAB TQ12 23 H2
Chapel St BUCKF TQ11 34 C4
TEIGN TQ14 21 F4
Chapple Cross BVYTR TQ13 6 D5
Chapple Rd BVYTR TQ13 6 C3
Charlemont Rd TEIGN TQ14 14 B5
Charles Rd NWTAB TQ12 38 C1
Charles St DART TQ6 71 F2
Charlotte Cl
SPH/CHEL/BTN TQ2 39 H3
Charmouth Cl TQ TQ1 40 D5
Chartwell Cl PAIGN TQ3 54 A2
Chatsworth Rd TQ TQ1 40 B5
Chatto Rd TQ TQ1 40 A4
Chatto Wy TQ TQ1 40 A4
Chelsea Pl TEIGN TQ14 21 F3
Chelston Rd NWTAB TQ12 23 F2
SPH/CHEL/BTN TQ2 4 B5
Chercombe Br NWTAB TQ12 22 A2
Chercombe Bridge Rd
NWTAB TQ12 22 A2
Chercombe Cl NWTAB TQ12 22 C1
Chercombe Valley Rd
NWTAB TQ12 22 C1
Cherry Brook Dr
GDRG/BDS TQ4 58 D4
Cherry Cross TOT TQ9 * 50 C5
Cherry Gdns PAIGN TQ3 2 D1
Cherry Park Cl
SPH/CHEL/BTN TQ2 47 F4
Cherrywood Cl NWTAB TQ12 22 C1
Chestnut Av DART TQ6 71 E1
SPH/CHEL/BTN TQ2 4 C3
Chestnut Dr BRIX TQ5 64 A5
NWTAB TQ12 24 C4
Chilcote Cl TQ TQ1 40 C3
Chiltern Cl SPH/CHEL/BTN TQ2 47 F3
Chilton Av TEIGN TQ14 21 G2
Chinkwell Ri
SPH/CHEL/BTN TQ2 38 D3
Chiseldon Farm BRIX TQ5 64 B5
Chiseldon Hl BRIX TQ5 64 C5
Christina Pk TOT TQ9 51 E4
Chudleigh Rd NWTAB TQ12 17 H2
Chuley Hl BVYTR TQ13 29 F5
Chuley Rd BVYTR TQ13 29 F4
Church Ct NWTAB TQ12 * 18 A4
Church Cross Rd BUCKF TQ11 34 C3
Church End Rd NWTAB TQ12 31 F4

Cl NWTAB TQ12 36 B1
g Cl BUCKF TQ11 34 C2
s Cl GDRG/BDS TQ4 58 C2
gh Cross TQ TQ1 40 C3
ap NWTAB TQ12 12 D5
own Rd NWTAB TQ12 31 G3
dns TOT TQ9 51 F4
ood PAIGN TQ3 45 H4
am Pk BRIX TQ5 64 B2
ill Rd TQ TQ1 40 A5
a BRIX TQ5 64 D2
eigh La BVYTR TQ13 7 F1
Rd TOT TQ9 51 F4

G

ll Hl NWTAB TQ12 33 G1
ll La NWTAB TQ12 33 F1
orough Cl TQ TQ1 48 D2
lery
/CHEL/BTN TQ2 * 5 H4
ay Dr TEIGN TQ14 20 D1
ton Farm Cl BRIX TQ5 62 D2
ton Gld BRIX TQ5 62 D2
SPH/CHEL/BTN TQ2 33 E5
Rd TQ TQ1 40 B5
d Pl TOT TQ9 * 50 C4
d Rd GDRG/BDS TQ4 3 G2
Rea BRIX TQ5 64 D2
s La NWTAB TQ12 22 B4
Cl BRIX TQ5 64 C4
n Av NWTAB TQ12 23 F1
Rd SPH/CHEL/BTN TQ2 40 A1
use Cl DAW EX7 8 D5
use Hl DAW EX7 8 D5
use Ri DAW EX7 8 D5
ee Cl NWTAB TQ12 18 B3
y La BRIX TQ5 68 D1
l NWTAB TQ12 16 D5
n Cl PAIGN TQ3 45 H4
Rd PAIGN TQ3 46 D5
St NWTAB TQ12 23 F2
N TQ14 21 G4
n Pl PAIGN TQ3 2 E2
n Rd GDRG/BDS TQ4 3 F3
rstons PAIGN TQ3 * 2 E2
ge Rd NWTAB TQ12 17 H3
Gdns GDRG/BDS TQ4 58 C3
Rd GDRG/BDS TQ4 58 C3
Av TEIGN TQ14 14 A5
Cl SPH/CHEL/BTN TQ2 39 F5
Rd NWTAB TQ12 24 A2
Wy GDRG/BDS TQ4 58 C2
Rd BRIX TQ5 65 E3
Cl DAW EX7 9 E4
one Ter TEIGN TQ14 21 G3
ate La GDRG/BDS TQ4 52 C3
Cl NWTAB TQ12 * 22 D2
ands BUCKF TQ11 34 B3
and Wy
/CHEL/BTN TQ2 38 D3
ebe NWTAB TQ12 36 A1
rnock Cl TQ TQ1 39 G4
le DART TQ6 * 61 H5
ragh Rd TEIGN TQ14 21 G3
ore Rd BRIX TQ5 64 C3
PAIGN TQ3 3 F1
le Cl TEIGN TQ14 21 F2
orne Cl TQ TQ1 48 D2
ster Cl
/CHEL/BTN TQ2 39 H2
ster Rd NWTAB TQ12 23 G3
N TQ14 21 F3
y Av PAIGN TQ3 46 D4
Cl BRIX TQ5 64 B5
Park Av
/CHEL/BTN TQ2 32 D4
ds BRIX TQ5 64 A2
ds Cl BRIX TQ5 64 B2
s Hill Cl NWTAB TQ12 18 A3
s Hill Rd NWTAB TQ12 18 A3
dge Cl DAW EX7 8 D4
ngton Orch
G/BDS TQ4 * 59 E2
ngton Rd
G/BDS TQ4 58 C3
y TEIGN TQ14 21 G2
n Rd
/CHEL/BTN TQ2 4 B2
Rd NWTAB TQ12 23 F3
Rd SALC TQ8 77 F2
ers La NWTAB TQ12 38 B1
n Rd TQ TQ1 5 H3
n Ter TQ TQ1 5 H3
n Rd PAIGN TQ3 46 C5
rcy Flds BRIX TQ5 64 B5
ian Cl GDRG/BDS TQ4 53 H5
son Av TEIGN TQ14 20 A2
Av GDRG/BDS TQ4 58 D2
Dr TEIGN TQ14 21 F2
Hts GDRG/BDS TQ4 58 C3
Heights Cl
G/BDS TQ4 58 C3
Rd BUCKF TQ11 34 B2
G/BDS TQ4 58 D3
AB TQ12 30 B2
Q1 5 K1
ere Cl TQ TQ1 40 B1
ns La TOT TQ9 42 D5
Furlong TEIGN TQ14 19 G2
Headland Crs
N TQ3 47 E5
Headland Rd PAIGN TQ3 47 E5
Hill Rd
/CHEL/BTN TQ2 32 D4
ark La PAIGN TQ3 53 H3
Parks Rd PAIGN TQ3 54 A4
Rea Rd BRIX TQ5 64 D2
or Cl PAIGN TQ3 46 B5
Western Cl
G/BDS TQ4 3 F6
Western Rd
G/BDS TQ4 3 F3
Western Wy
AB TQ12 * 23 H1
eebys PAIGN TQ3 2 D2
away La NWTAB TQ12 31 H2

Greenaway Rd NWTAB TQ12 23 E1
Greenbank Av NWTAB TQ12 17 H3
Greenbank Rd BRIX TQ5 64 B3
Green Cl KING TQ7 75 F2
Greenfield Rd PAIGN TQ3 46 C4
Greenhill Gdns NWTAB TQ12 31 F4
Greenhill Rd NWTAB TQ12 18 A4
NWTAB TQ12 31 F4
Greenhill Wy NWTAB TQ12 18 A4
Greenlands Av PAIGN TQ3 2 B3
Green La BRIX TQ5 63 G2
BUCKF TQ11 35 F5
Greenover Cl BRIX TQ5 64 B4
Greenover Rd BRIX TQ5 64 B4
Green Park Rd PAIGN TQ3 46 B5
Greenswood Rd BRIX TQ5 64 C4
The Green TEIGN TQ14 21 E5
Greenway Cl
SPH/CHEL/BTN TQ2 40 A2
Greenway Gdns
SPH/CHEL/BTN TQ2 40 A1
Greenway La TQ TQ1 40 B3
Greenway Pk BRIX TQ5 62 D3
Greenway Rd BRIX TQ5 62 A5
SPH/CHEL/BTN TQ2 47 F2
Greenway Ter TQ TQ1 * 40 B3
Grenville Av
SPH/CHEL/BTN TQ2 39 F5
TEIGN TQ14 21 E1
Grenville Cl DART TQ6 70 D2
NWTAB TQ12 24 A2
Grenville Rd SALC TQ8 77 F3
Grenville Wy GDRG/BDS TQ4 58 D2
Greycoat La NWTAB TQ12 16 D3
Greystone Wy TQ TQ1 40 B4
Gropers La NWTAB TQ12 37 F2
Grosvenor Av
SPH/CHEL/BTN TQ2 39 E3
Grosvenor Cl
SPH/CHEL/BTN TQ2 39 E2
Grosvenor Rd GDRG/BDS TQ4 2 E4
Grosvenor Ter GDRG/BDS TQ4 2 E4
Grove Cl TOT TQ9 50 C4
Grove Ct DAW EX7 9 E5
TEIGN TQ14 21 G2
Grove Crs TEIGN TQ14 21 F3
Grove Ms TOT TQ9 50 C4
Grove Ter TEIGN TQ14 21 F3
The Grove GDRG/BDS TQ4 54 A5
TOT TQ9 50 C4
Guestland Rd TQ TQ1 40 B2
Guildhall Yd TOT TQ9 50 C3
The Gurneys PAIGN TQ3 2 C4

H

Haccombe Pth NWTAB TQ12 24 C4
Hackney La NWTAB TQ12 18 B4
Halcyon Rd NWTAB TQ12 23 F2
Haldon Av TEIGN TQ14 21 G2
Haldon Cl TQ TQ1 49 E2
Haldon Rd TQ TQ1 48 D2
Hall La DAW EX7 15 E5
Hall's La NWTAB TQ12 31 F4
Halsteads Rd
SPH/CHEL/BTN TQ2 40 A1
Hambleton Wy
GDRG/BDS TQ4 58 C2
Hameldown Cl
SPH/CHEL/BTN TQ2 38 C4
Hamelin Wy
SPH/CHEL/BTN TQ2 38 C2
Hamilton Dr NWTAB TQ12 23 F1
The Hamiltons TEIGN TQ14 * 21 E5
Ham La DART TQ6 61 G4
TEIGN TQ14 26 D1
Hampton Av TQ TQ1 40 C3
Hampton La TQ TQ1 40 C3
Hanover Cl BRIX TQ5 64 C4
Happaway Cl
SPH/CHEL/BTN TQ2 40 A1
Happaway Rd
SPH/CHEL/BTN TQ2 40 A1
Happy Va TEIGN TQ14 * 19 F2
Harberton Cl GDRG/BDS TQ4 58 A1
Harbourne Av GDRG/BDS TQ4 58 A1
Harbour View Cl BRIX TQ5 64 C2
Hardness Cl DART TQ6 70 C3
Hardy Cl TQ TQ1 5 K7
Hares La BVYTR TQ13 29 F3
Harper's Hl TOT TQ9 50 A5
Hart Land Tor Cl BRIX TQ5 64 A5
Hartley Rd GDRG/BDS TQ4 2 C5
Hartop Rd TQ TQ1 40 B2
Harts Cl TEIGN TQ14 21 E2
Haslam Rd TQ TQ1 40 A4
Hatchcombe La
SPH/CHEL/BTN TQ2 39 H1
Hatcher St DAW EX7 15 F1
Hatfield Rd TQ TQ1 40 A5
Hauley Rd DART TQ6 71 F2
Havelock Rd TQ TQ1 40 B2
The Haven TEIGN TQ14 19 H3
Hawarden Ter DART TQ6 * 71 H2
Hawkes Wy TOT TQ9 * 50 C4
Hawkins Av
SPH/CHEL/BTN TQ2 39 E4
Hawkins Dr TEIGN TQ14 21 F2
Hawkins Rd NWTAB TQ12 24 B2
Hawthorn Cl KING TQ7 75 E4
Hawthorne Cl NWTAB TQ12 24 B5
Hawthorn Park Cl
SPH/CHEL/BTN TQ2 47 F3
Hayes Cl TOT TQ9 51 E5
Hayes Gdns GDRG/BDS TQ4 2 C5
Hayes Rd GDRG/BDS TQ4 2 B6
Hayle Av GDRG/BDS TQ4 58 D4
Hayley Pk NWTAB TQ12 31 F5
Hayton Cl TEIGN TQ14 20 D2
Haytor Av GDRG/BDS TQ4 58 B1
Haytor Dr NWTAB TQ12 24 B2
Haytor Gv NWTAB TQ12 24 C2
Haytor Pk NWTAB TQ12 18 A3
Haytor Rd TQ TQ1 40 B4
Haywain Cl
SPH/CHEL/BTN TQ2 38 D3
Hazelbank DART TQ6 * 71 G2

Hazel Cl KING TQ7 75 E4
TEIGN TQ14 14 B5
Hazeldown Rd TEIGN TQ14 21 F1
Hazelwood Cl BRIX TQ5 * 64 D3
Hazelwood Dr DAW EX7 9 F2
Headborough Rd BVYTR TQ13 28 D3
Headland Gv PAIGN TQ3 47 E5
Headland Park Rd PAIGN TQ3 47 E5
Headland Rd
SPH/CHEL/BTN TQ2 47 G4
The Headlands
SPH/CHEL/BTN TQ2 * 47 G4
Headway Cl TEIGN TQ14 20 D3
Headway Cross Rd
TEIGN TQ14 20 D2
Headway Ri TEIGN TQ14 20 D2
Heather Cl NWTAB TQ12 22 D1
TEIGN TQ14 21 F1
Heather Wy BRIX TQ5 63 H3
Heathfield Cl BVYTR TQ13 7 E5
Heathfield Meadow
BVYTR TQ13 7 E5
Heathfield Ter BVYTR TQ13 * 7 E4
Heath Hl NWTAB TQ12 11 E3
Heath Pk BRIX TQ5 64 D2
NWTAB TQ12 24 C4
Heath Ri BRIX TQ5 * 65 E2
Heath Rd BRIX TQ5 65 E2
Heaviside Cl
SPH/CHEL/BTN TQ2 33 F5
Helens Mead Cl
SPH/CHEL/BTN TQ2 33 E4
Helens Mead Rd
SPH/CHEL/BTN TQ2 33 E4
Hele Rd NWTAB TQ12 17 H1
SPH/CHEL/BTN TQ2 39 G3
Helford Dr GDRG/BDS TQ4 58 D4
Heligan Dr PAIGN TQ3 54 A2
Hellevoetsluis Wy PAIGN TQ3 46 A2
Helmdon Ri
SPH/CHEL/BTN TQ2 38 D3
Helston Cl PAIGN TQ3 2 A1
Hembury Cock Hl BUCKF TQ11 34 B2
Hembury Pk BUCKF TQ11 34 C2
Henacre Rd KING TQ7 75 F3
Henbury Cl TQ TQ1 40 B5
Hennapyn Rd
SPH/CHEL/BTN TQ2 4 B6
Hennock Rd GDRG/BDS TQ4 58 B2
Hensford Rd DAW EX7 8 A1
Henty Av DAW EX7 9 E5
Henty Cl DAW EX7 9 E4
Herbert Rd SALC TQ8 77 F3
SPH/CHEL/BTN TQ2 47 F2
Hermitage Rd DART TQ6 70 D1
Hermosa Gdns TEIGN TQ14 21 F3
Hermosa Rd TEIGN TQ14 21 F3
Heron Wy SPH/CHEL/BTN TQ2 32 A5
Hesketh Crs TQ TQ1 48 D3
Hesketh Ms TQ TQ1 * 48 D3
Hesketh Rd TQ TQ1 48 D3
Hestow Rd NWTAB TQ12 13 E5
Hewitt Cl NWTAB TQ12 24 C3
Heywood Est NWTAB TQ12 * 17 H4
Heywoods Rd TEIGN TQ14 21 G3
Highcliffe Ms GDRG/BDS TQ4 3 H6
High Cl BVYTR TQ13 7 G3
Higher Audley Av
SPH/CHEL/BTN TQ2 39 H3
Higher Bibbery BVYTR TQ13 7 G3
Higher Brimley Rd TEIGN TQ14 21 F2
Higher Buckeridge Rd
TEIGN TQ14 21 F1
Higher Budleigh Meadow
NWTAB TQ12 22 D2
Higher Cadewell La
SPH/CHEL/BTN TQ2 38 D2
Higher Contour Rd DART TQ6 71 H2
Higher Coombe Dr
TEIGN TQ14 21 E1
Higher Copythorne BRIX TQ5 64 A3
Higher Downs Rd TQ TQ1 40 C3
Higher Dr DAW EX7 9 E4
Higher Edginswell La
SPH/CHEL/BTN TQ2 38 C4
Higher Erith Rd TQ TQ1 48 D2
Higher Furzeham Rd
BRIX TQ5 64 C1
Higher Holcombe Cl
TEIGN TQ14 21 G1
Higher Holcombe Dr
TEIGN TQ14 14 C5
Higher Holcombe Rd
TEIGN TQ14 14 C5
Higher Kingsdown Rd
TEIGN TQ14 20 D3
Higher Lincombe Rd TQ TQ1 48 D3
Higher Manor Rd BRIX TQ5 64 C2
Higher Manor Ter PAIGN TQ3 2 C4
Higher Mill La BUCKF TQ11 34 C3
Higher Penn BRIX TQ5 64 D4
Higher Polsham Rd PAIGN TQ3 54 D2
Higher Queens Ter TQ TQ1 5 H2
Higher Ramshill La PAIGN TQ3 53 F1
Higher Ranscombe Rd
BRIX TQ5 64 D3
Higher Ringmore Rd
TEIGN TQ14 26 D1
Higher Roborough
BVYTR TQ13 29 G3
Higher Rydons BRIX TQ5 64 A3
Higher Sackery NWTAB TQ12 25 F1
Higher Steps BRIX TQ5 * 64 C2
Higher St DART TQ6 61 F5
DART TQ6 71 F2
Higher Union La
SPH/CHEL/BTN TQ2 4 E1
Higher Union Rd KING TQ7 75 E3
Higher Warberry Rd TQ TQ1 5 K2
Higher Warborough Rd
BRIX TQ5 62 D1
Higher Warren Rd KING TQ7 75 G5
Higher Westonfields TOT TQ9 51 E4
Higher Woodfield Rd TQ TQ1 5 K5
Higher Woodway Rd
TEIGN TQ14 14 B4
Higher Yannon Dr TEIGN TQ14 21 E2
Highfield Cl BRIX TQ5 64 A3
Highfield Crs PAIGN TQ3 54 A3
Highfield Dr KING TQ7 75 F4

Highgrove Pk TEIGN TQ14 21 G1
High House Cl DAW EX7 8 D5
High House La KING TQ7 75 F4
Highland Cl
SPH/CHEL/BTN TQ2 39 E5
Highland Rd
SPH/CHEL/BTN TQ2 39 E5
High St DAW EX7 15 G1
TOT TQ9 50 C4
Highweek Rd NWTAB TQ12 23 E2
Highweek St NWTAB TQ12 23 F1
Highweek Village
NWTAB TQ12 16 D5
Highwood Cl NWTAB TQ12 * 23 F3
Hillbrook Ri TOT TQ9 51 E4
Hillbrook Rd TOT TQ9 51 E4
Hilldown TOT TQ9 51 E4
Hilldrop Ter TQ TQ1 * 5 G2
Hiller La NWTAB TQ12 25 E2
Hillesdon Rd TQ TQ1 5 H3
Hillfield TOT TQ9 56 D5
Hillhead Pk BRIX TQ5 68 C2
Hillmans Rd NWTAB TQ12 23 G3
Hill Park Cl BRIX TQ5 65 E3
Hill Park Rd BRIX TQ5 65 E3
NWTAB TQ12 22 D1
TQ TQ1 40 A4
Hill Park Ter GDRG/BDS TQ4 3 G4
Hillrise BRIX TQ5 62 D2
Hill Rd NWTAB TQ12 23 F3
Hillside Cl TEIGN TQ14 20 D1
Hillside Dr KING TQ7 75 F4
Hillside Rd BRIX TQ5 64 C3
PAIGN TQ3 2 B1
Hillside Ter DART TQ6 * 71 G2
PAIGN TQ3 * 2 D2
Hilly Gardens Rd TQ TQ1 40 B2
Hilton Crs PAIGN TQ3 47 E4
Hilton Dr PAIGN TQ3 47 E5
Hilton Rd NWTAB TQ12 23 G3
Hind St BVYTR TQ13 7 F2
Hingston Rd TQ TQ1 40 C5
Hodson Cl PAIGN TQ3 54 B2
Hoile La TOT TQ9 56 C4
Holbeam Cl NWTAB TQ12 22 C1
Holborn Rd BRIX TQ5 64 C1
Holcombe Down Rd
TEIGN TQ14 14 C3
Holcombe Dr DAW EX7 15 F5
Holcombe Rd DAW EX7 15 E4
Hollacombe La PAIGN TQ3 47 F5
Hollam Wy NWTAB TQ12 18 B2
Hollywater Cl TQ TQ1 48 D1
Holman Cl DAW EX7 9 E4
Holne Moor Cl PAIGN TQ3 54 A2
Holne Rd BUCKF TQ11 34 B2
Holwell Rd BRIX TQ5 64 B3
Holwill Tor Wk GDRG/BDS TQ4 58 B1
Home Cl BRIX TQ5 64 C4
Homelands Rd KING TQ7 75 E2
Homers Cl NWTAB TQ12 17 H4
Homers Crs NWTAB TQ12 17 H4
Homers La NWTAB TQ12 17 H4
Homestead Rd TQ TQ1 40 A3
Homestead Ter TQ TQ1 * 40 A3
Honey La NWTAB TQ12 32 D2
Honeysuckle Cl PAIGN TQ3 54 A1
Honeywell Rd NWTAB TQ12 18 A4
Hoodown La DART TQ6 71 G2
Hookhills Dr GDRG/BDS TQ4 59 E3
Hookhills Gdns GDRG/BDS TQ4 58 D5
Hookhills Gv GDRG/BDS TQ4 59 E3
Hookhills Rd GDRG/BDS TQ4 58 D4
Hope Cl TOT TQ9 51 F4
Hope's Cl TEIGN TQ14 21 E2
Hopkins La NWTAB TQ12 23 G2
Horace Rd SPH/CHEL/BTN TQ2 39 H1
Horns Pk TEIGN TQ14 19 G3
Horse La TEIGN TQ14 21 F5
Horsepool St BRIX TQ5 64 B4
Horseshoe Bend
GDRG/BDS TQ4 59 E2
Hosegood Wy NWTAB TQ12 17 H3
Hoskings Ct BUCKF TQ11 34 C4
Hospital Hl DAW EX7 15 F1
Hospital La BVYTR TQ13 29 G2
Hound Tor Cl GDRG/BDS TQ4 58 D5
Howard Cl SPH/CHEL/BTN TQ2 39 F5
TEIGN TQ14 21 E1
Howards Wy NWTAB TQ12 24 A2
Howton Rd NWTAB TQ12 16 B5
Hoxton Rd TQ TQ1 5 H1
Hoyle's Rd PAIGN TQ3 54 A1
Huccaby Cl BRIX TQ5 63 H5
Humber La NWTAB TQ12 18 B2
The Humpy DAW EX7 8 B5
Hunsdon Rd TQ TQ1 5 J3
Huntacott Wy
SPH/CHEL/BTN TQ2 38 D3
Hunters Tor Dr GDRG/BDS TQ4 58 D5
Hutchings Wy TEIGN TQ14 20 D2
Hutton Rd PAIGN TQ3 46 C5
Huxley V NWTAB TQ12 31 E5
Huxnor Rd NWTAB TQ12 31 F5
Hyde Rd GDRG/BDS TQ4 3 F2
Hyfield Gdns TQ TQ1 * 5 H3

I

Idewell Rd SPH/CHEL/BTN TQ2 40 B1
Ilbert Rd KING TQ7 75 E3
Ilsham Cl TQ TQ1 49 F1
Ilsham Crs TQ TQ1 49 F1
Ilsham Marine Dr TQ TQ1 49 F2
Ilsham Ms TQ TQ1 * 49 E1
Ilsham Rd TQ TQ1 49 E1
Ilton Wy KING TQ7 75 F3
Indio Rd BVYTR TQ13 7 E4
Innerbrook Rd
SPH/CHEL/BTN TQ2 4 B1
Inverteign Dr TEIGN TQ14 20 D3
Ipplepen Rd NWTAB TQ12 37 F5
PAIGN TQ3 45 G2
Isaac Gv SPH/CHEL/BTN TQ2 32 D5
Isaacs Rd SPH/CHEL/BTN TQ2 32 D5
Isambard Ct
SPH/CHEL/BTN TQ2 33 F5

Isigny Rd KING TQ7 75 E3
Island St SALC TQ8 77 F2
Island Ter SALC TQ8 77 G2
Ivatt Rd DART TQ6 70 C2
Ivy La TEIGN TQ14 21 F4
Ivy Tree Hl NWTAB TQ12 26 A3

J

Jack's La SPH/CHEL/BTN TQ2 32 D5
Jacolind Wk BRIX TQ5 64 D2
James Av PAIGN TQ3 46 A5
Jasmine Gv PAIGN TQ3 54 A1
Jawbones Hl DART TQ6 71 E3
Jetty Marsh Rd NWTAB TQ12 23 F1
Jews Br NWTAB TQ12 11 F2
John Acres La NWTAB TQ12 12 B2
John Nash Dr DAW EX7 15 E2
Jonida Cl TQ TQ1 40 A4
Jordan Dr TEIGN TQ14 20 D2
Jordan St BUCKF TQ11 34 B4
Jubilee Cl DART TQ6 70 C2
Jubilee Rd NWTAB TQ12 23 F2
TOT TQ9 51 E3
Jubilee Ter DART TQ6 * 71 H2
PAIGN TQ3 2 D2
Jurys Corner Cl NWTAB TQ12 31 G4

K

Keatings La TEIGN TQ14 21 E3
Keats Cl TEIGN TQ14 20 D1
The Keep Gdns DART TQ6 71 E2
Keep La DART TQ6 71 E1
Kelland Cl PAIGN TQ3 2 B3
Kellett Cl BVYTR TQ13 29 G3
Kellock Dr TOT TQ9 50 B4
Kelly Cl TQ TQ1 5 K7
Kemmings Cl GDRG/BDS TQ4 58 B3
Kennels Rd BRIX TQ5 63 E4
Kenneth Ct
SPH/CHEL/BTN TQ2 39 E3
Kensey Cl TQ TQ1 41 E5
Kent's La TQ TQ1 49 E1
Kents Rd TQ TQ1 49 E1
Kenwith Dr KING TQ7 75 F3
Kenwyn Rd TQ TQ1 40 C5
Kernou Rd GDRG/BDS TQ4 3 G3
Kerria Cl PAIGN TQ3 54 A1
Kestor Dr PAIGN TQ3 46 C4
Keyberry Mi NWTAB TQ12 * 24 A4
Keyberry Pk NWTAB TQ12 23 H4
Keyberry Rd NWTAB TQ12 23 H4
Keysfield Rd GDRG/BDS TQ4 3 G5
Killerton Cl PAIGN TQ3 2 E1
Kilmorie Cl TQ TQ1 49 F3
Kiln Cl BVYTR TQ13 7 E5
Kilnford Rd NWTAB TQ12 18 B3
Kiln Orch NWTAB TQ12 22 D2
Kiln Pth BRIX TQ5 64 C3
Kiln Rd BVYTR TQ13 7 E5
PAIGN TQ3 45 G3
Kingcome Ct BUCKF TQ11 34 D4
Kingfisher Cl
SPH/CHEL/BTN TQ2 39 F1
Kingsale Rd SALC TQ8 77 E3
King's Ash Rd PAIGN TQ3 54 A2
Kingsbridge Hl TOT TQ9 50 C5
Kings Coombe Dr
NWTAB TQ12 18 A1
Kings Ct NWTAB TQ12 18 A4
NWTAB TQ12 * 31 F4
Kingsdown Cl DAW EX7 8 D5
TEIGN TQ14 20 D3
Kingsdown Crs DAW EX7 8 D5
Kingsdown Rd TEIGN TQ14 20 D3
Kings Dr BRIX TQ5 64 D3
The Kings Dr
SPH/CHEL/BTN TQ2 4 C3
Kingsgate Cl
SPH/CHEL/BTN TQ2 33 F4
Kingshurst Dr PAIGN TQ3 54 D1
Kingskerswell Rd
NWTAB TQ12 23 H5
SPH/CHEL/BTN TQ2 32 C5
Kingskerwell Rd
SPH/CHEL/BTN TQ2 39 E2
Kingsland Av GDRG/BDS TQ4 54 A5
Kingsland Dr GDRG/BDS TQ4 54 A5
Kingsley Av
SPH/CHEL/BTN TQ2 32 D5
Kingsley Rd KING TQ7 75 E4
Kings Orch TOT TQ9 51 E4
King's Quay DART TQ6 71 F1
Kings Rd PAIGN TQ3 55 E2
Kings Rydon Cl TOT TQ9 56 D4
Kingsteignton Rd
NWTAB TQ12 23 G1
Kingston Cl NWTAB TQ12 31 G3
Kingston La DART TQ6 70 D2
King St BRIX TQ5 64 D2
DAW EX7 15 F1
NWTAB TQ12 23 G2
Kingswater Ct BRIX TQ5 64 C2
Kingsway TEIGN TQ14 20 D3
Kingsway Av GDRG/BDS TQ4 58 C3
Kingsway Cl GDRG/BDS TQ4 58 C3
KING TQ7 75 E4
Kingsway Dr GDRG/BDS TQ4 58 B3
Kingsway Pk KING TQ7 75 E4
Kingswear Rd BRIX TQ5 68 D2
Kintyre Cl SPH/CHEL/BTN TQ2 32 C5
Kirkham St PAIGN TQ3 2 D2
Kirkstead Cl
SPH/CHEL/BTN TQ2 39 G3
Kirtons Rd NWTAB TQ12 33 F1
Kittersley Dr NWTAB TQ12 10 B5
Kittiwake Dr
SPH/CHEL/BTN TQ2 39 E1
Knapp Park Rd
GDRG/BDS TQ4 59 E2
Knick Knack La BRIX TQ5 64 C4
Knowle Cl BVYTR TQ13 28 D4
Knowle Gdns KING TQ7 75 E2

Knowle House Cl KING TQ7 75 E2
Knowle Rd SALC TQ8 77 F2
Knowles Hill Rd NWTAB TQ12 23 F1

L

Laburnam Ter NWTAB TQ12 30 B1
Laburnham Gv TOT TQ9 50 A2
Laburnum Rd NWTAB TQ12 24 A4
Laburnum Rw
SPH/CHEL/BTN TQ2 4 D1
Laburnum St
SPH/CHEL/BTN TQ2 4 D1
Lacy Rd PAIGN TQ3 46 C5
Lady Park Rd
SPH/CHEL/BTN TQ2 47 F3
Lady's Mile DAW EX7 * 9 F5
Lake Av TEIGN TQ14 21 E1
Lakes Cl BRIX TQ5 64 A3
Lakeside DAW EX7 9 F2
SALC TQ8 77 F2
Lakeside Cl BVYTR TQ13 10 A1
Lakes Rd BRIX TQ5 64 A3
Lake St DART TQ6 71 F2
Lamacraft Cl DAW EX7 9 E4
Lambert Cl DAW EX7 9 E4
Lambert's La TEIGN TQ14 26 D1
Lammas La PAIGN TQ3 54 B1
Lancaster Dr GDRG/BDS TQ4 58 B2
Landmark Rd SALC TQ8 76 D3
Landscore Cl TEIGN TQ14 21 F3
Landscore Rd TEIGN TQ14 21 E3
Landsdowne Pk TOT TQ9 51 E5
Lands Rd BRIX TQ5 65 E1
The Lane DART TQ6 61 G5
Langaller Cl BVYTR TQ13 6 D5
Langdon Flds BRIX TQ5 62 D1
Langdon La BRIX TQ5 62 D1
Langdon Rd DAW EX7 8 C4
PAIGN TQ3 47 E5
Langford Br NWTAB TQ12 31 E1
Langford Crs
SPH/CHEL/BTN TQ2 32 D5
Langlands Cl GDRG/BDS TQ4 54 A5
Langley Av BRIX TQ5 64 C3
Langley Cl BRIX TQ5 64 C3
Langridge Rd PAIGN TQ3 54 A1
Langs Rd PAIGN TQ3 55 E1
Langstone Cl NWTAB TQ12 10 D3
TQ TQ1 40 D4
Lang Wy NWTAB TQ12 36 C1
Lansdowne La
SPH/CHEL/BTN TQ2 4 C1
Lansdowne Rd
SPH/CHEL/BTN TQ2 4 C1
Larks Cl TEIGN TQ14 26 D1
Larksmead Wy NWTAB TQ12 22 D4
Laskeys Heath NWTAB TQ12 10 A5
Laura Av PAIGN TQ3 54 D1
Laura Gv PAIGN TQ3 54 C1
Laurel La TEIGN TQ14 20 D5
Laurie Av NWTAB TQ12 22 D1
Lavender Cl BRIX TQ5 64 A3
Lawn Cl SPH/CHEL/BTN TQ2 32 D5
Lawn Hl DAW EX7 15 G1
Lawns End TEIGN TQ14 19 G3
The Lawn DAW EX7 * 15 G1
Lawrence Pl
SPH/CHEL/BTN TQ2 * 5 H4
Laywell Cl BRIX TQ5 64 B5
Laywell Rd BRIX TQ5 64 A4
Leader La PAIGN TQ3 45 H5
Lealands BVYTR TQ13 7 E4
Lea Mt TEIGN TQ14 20 A2
Lea Mount Cl DAW EX7 15 F2
Lea Mount Dr DAW EX7 15 F2
Lea Mount Rd DAW EX7 15 G2
Lea Rd SPH/CHEL/BTN TQ2 33 E5
The Lea TEIGN TQ14 20 B2
Leathe Ter NWTAB TQ12 * 18 A3
Leat Meadow NWTAB TQ12 10 B5
Leaze Rd NWTAB TQ12 17 H2
Ledsgrove NWTAB TQ12 36 C1
Leechwell La TOT TQ9 50 C4
Leechwell St TOT TQ9 50 B4
Leeward La
SPH/CHEL/BTN TQ2 32 C5
Leigham Ct DAW EX7 15 G1
Leighon Rd GDRG/BDS TQ4 3 G2
Lembury Rd TOT TQ9 56 D3
Le Molay-Littry Wy
BVYTR TQ13 7 F3
Lemon Rd NWTAB TQ12 23 G2
The Level DART TQ6 61 G5
Leyburn Gv GDRG/BDS TQ4 2 C6
Ley La NWTAB TQ12 17 H2
Leys Rd SPH/CHEL/BTN TQ2 47 F1
Lichfield Av
SPH/CHEL/BTN TQ2 39 H2
Lichfield Cl BRIX TQ5 64 A3
Lichfield Dr BRIX TQ5 64 A3
Lidford Tor Av GDRG/BDS TQ4 58 A1
Light La BRIX TQ5 62 D3
Lime Av SPH/CHEL/BTN TQ2 4 C2
Lime Gv KING TQ7 75 E3
Lime Grove Ter
SPH/CHEL/BTN TQ2 * 4 D2
Lime Tree Wk NWTAB TQ12 24 A4
Linacre La NWTAB TQ12 32 A2
Linacre Rd SPH/CHEL/BTN TQ2 32 D5
Lincoln Gn SPH/CHEL/BTN TQ2 40 A2
Lincombe Dr TQ TQ1 49 E2
Lincombe Hill Dr TQ TQ1 48 D3
Lincombe Hill Rd TQ TQ1 49 E2
Linden Rd DAW EX7 15 E2
Linden Ter NWTAB TQ12 23 E2
Lindfield Cl
SPH/CHEL/BTN TQ2 39 H3
Lindisfarne Wy
SPH/CHEL/BTN TQ2 39 G1
Lindridge Cl NWTAB TQ12 13 E5
Lindridge Hl NWTAB TQ12 13 E5
Lindridge La NWTAB TQ12 12 D5
Lindridge Rd TQ TQ1 40 C3
Lindsay Rd PAIGN TQ3 46 C4
Lindthorpe Wy BRIX TQ5 64 B3
Linhay Cl BRIX TQ5 68 D2
Linhey Cl KING TQ7 75 F5
Links Cl BRIX TQ5 63 G1
Lion Cl KING TQ7 75 E3
Lisburne Crs TQ TQ1 48 D2
Lisburne Pl TQ TQ1 * 48 D2
Lisburne Sq TQ TQ1 48 D2
Little Barton NWTAB TQ12 18 A1
Little Bossell La BUCKF TQ11 34 C5
Little Cl NWTAB TQ12 18 A1
Littlefield TEIGN TQ14 19 G2
Littlefield Cl
SPH/CHEL/BTN TQ2 39 F2
Littlegate Rd PAIGN TQ3 2 E2
Little Hl SALC TQ8 77 E2
Littlejoy Rd NWTAB TQ12 22 A1
Little Park Rd PAIGN TQ3 2 C2
Little Week Cl DAW EX7 9 E3
Little Week Gdns DAW EX7 9 E3
Littleweek La DAW EX7 9 E3
Little Week Rd DAW EX7 9 E3
Livermead Hl
SPH/CHEL/BTN TQ2 4 B7
Livingstone Rd TEIGN TQ14 21 G2
Lloyd Av SPH/CHEL/BTN TQ2 39 F4
Locarno Av PAIGN TQ3 47 F5
Locks Cl TQ TQ1 40 D4
Locks Hl TQ TQ1 40 D5
Locksley Cl TQ TQ1 40 B4
Logan Rd PAIGN TQ3 55 E2
Long Barton NWTAB TQ12 18 A1
Longcroft Av BRIX TQ5 64 B4
Longcroft Dr BRIX TQ5 64 B4
Longfield Dr SALC TQ8 77 E2
Longfields KING TQ7 74 C4
Longford La NWTAB TQ12 18 A2
Longford Pk NWTAB TQ12 18 A2
Longlands DAW EX7 15 E1
Long La DAW EX7 8 A3
NWTAB TQ12 24 D5
TEIGN TQ14 26 C2
Longmead Rd PAIGN TQ3 46 B5
Longpark Hl TQ TQ1 33 G2
Long Rd GDRG/BDS TQ4 57 G2
Long Rydon TOT TQ9 56 D4
Longstone Rd GDRG/BDS TQ4 54 A5
Long Wools GDRG/BDS TQ4 59 F5
Lonsdale Rd NWTAB TQ12 23 H3
Lords Pl TQ TQ1 40 B5
Loring Rd SALC TQ8 77 F3
Lorrie Dr TEIGN TQ14 21 E2
Louville Cl GDRG/BDS TQ4 59 E2
Love La BVYTR TQ13 29 F4
PAIGN TQ3 45 H2
Love Lane Cl PAIGN TQ3 45 H2
Loventor La TOT TQ9 45 E3
Lower Audley Rd
SPH/CHEL/BTN TQ2 39 H4
Lower Blagdon La PAIGN TQ3 53 G3
Lower Brimley Cl TEIGN TQ14 21 G3
Lower Brimley Rd TEIGN TQ14 21 G2
Lower Broad Pk DART TQ6 70 D2
Lower Broad Pth TOT TQ9 57 E5
Lower Brook St TEIGN TQ14 21 G3
Lower Cannon Rd
NWTAB TQ12 10 D3
Lower Collapark TOT TQ9 50 B3
Lower Collins Rd TOT TQ9 50 B3
Lower Contour Rd DART TQ6 71 H2
Lowerdown BVYTR TQ13 6 A2
Lower Dr DAW EX7 9 E4
Lower Ellacombe Church Rd
TQ TQ1 40 C5
Lower Erith Rd TQ TQ1 48 D2
Lower Fairview Rd DART TQ6 71 E2
Lower Fern Rd NWTAB TQ12 24 B5
Lower Fowden
GDRG/BDS TQ4 63 F1
Lower Kingsdown Rd
TEIGN TQ14 20 D3
Lower Manor Rd BRIX TQ5 64 C2
Lower Meadow Ri DAW EX7 15 E1
Lower Pk PAIGN TQ3 * 2 D1
Lower Penns Rd PAIGN TQ3 47 E5
Lower Polsham Rd PAIGN TQ3 3 F1
Lower Preston NWTAB TQ12 12 B5
Lower Rea Rd BRIX TQ5 64 D2
Lower Shirburn Rd TQ TQ1 40 A4
Lower St DART TQ6 61 F4
DART TQ6 71 F2
KING TQ7 74 C4
Lower Thurlow Rd TQ TQ1 40 A5
Lower Union La
SPH/CHEL/BTN TQ2 5 F2
Lower Union Rd KING TQ7 75 E3
Lower Warberry Rd TQ TQ1 5 H2
Lower Warren Rd KING TQ7 75 F5
Lower Woodfield Rd TQ TQ1 5 K5
Lower Yalberton Rd
GDRG/BDS TQ4 57 G2
Loxbury Ri
SPH/CHEL/BTN TQ2 47 F2
Loxbury Rd
SPH/CHEL/BTN TQ2 47 F2
Lucius St SPH/CHEL/BTN TQ2 4 D2
Lulworth Cl GDRG/BDS TQ4 58 B2
Lummaton Cross
SPH/CHEL/BTN TQ2 40 A1
Lummaton Pl
SPH/CHEL/BTN TQ2 40 B2
Luscombe Cl NWTAB TQ12 36 B2
Luscombe Crs PAIGN TQ3 54 A3
Luscombe Hl DAW EX7 14 B1
Luscombe La PAIGN TQ3 53 H1
Luscombe Rd PAIGN TQ3 53 H2
Luscombe Ter DAW EX7 15 F1
Lutyens Dr PAIGN TQ3 53 H2
Luxton Rd NWTAB TQ12 22 D5
Lydwell Park Rd TQ TQ1 40 D5
Lydwell Rd TQ TQ1 40 D5
Lyme Bay Rd TEIGN TQ14 21 F1
Lyme View Rd TQ TQ1 40 D4
Lymington Rd TQ TQ1 39 H4
Lyncombe Crs TQ TQ1 * 49 E3
Lyndale Rd NWTAB TQ12 17 H2
Lyndhurst Av NWTAB TQ12 31 G3
Lyndhurst Cl NWTAB TQ12 31 G2
Lyn Gv NWTAB TQ12 31 F2
Lynmouth Av GDRG/BDS TQ4 58 B2
Lyte Hill La
SPH/CHEL/BTN TQ2 32 D5
Lyte's Rd BRIX TQ5 64 D3

M

Mabel Pl GDRG/BDS TQ4 2 E4
Mackrells Ter NWTAB TQ12 * 23 E3
Maddacombe Rd NWTAB TQ12 30 D4
Maddicks Orch TOT TQ9 56 D5
Madeira Pl
SPH/CHEL/BTN TQ2 4 E2
Madrepore Pl TQ TQ1 5 G2
Madrepore Rd TQ TQ1 5 G3
Magdalene Cl TOT TQ9 50 C4
Magdalene Rd TQ TQ1 40 A5
Maidenway La PAIGN TQ3 54 B1
Maidenway Rd PAIGN TQ3 54 B1
Main Av TQ TQ1 40 A3
Main Rd SALC TQ8 77 E3
Malborough Pk KING TQ7 76 A1
Malderek Av PAIGN TQ3 47 E5
Mallands Meadow
NWTAB TQ12 30 A2
Mallard Cl SPH/CHEL/BTN TQ2 32 B5
Mallock Rd
SPH/CHEL/BTN TQ2 4 B2
Malting Ct DAW EX7 * 15 G1
Malt Ml TOT TQ9 50 B3
Manaton Tor Rd PAIGN TQ3 46 B5
Mannings Meadow
BVYTR TQ13 7 F3
Manor Av PAIGN TQ3 55 E1
Manor Bend BRIX TQ5 63 E1
Manor Cl NWTAB TQ12 30 A1
Manor Cnr PAIGN TQ3 * 55 E1
Manor Crs PAIGN TQ3 55 E1
Manor Dr NWTAB TQ12 31 G5
Manor Gdn TQ TQ1 49 E3
Manor Gdns NWTAB TQ12 30 B2
PAIGN TQ3 55 E1
TQ TQ1 * 49 E3
Manor Pk KING TQ7 75 F2
Manor Rd NWTAB TQ12 22 D1
PAIGN TQ3 55 E1
TEIGN TQ14 19 H2
TQ TQ1 40 B3
Manor Rw DAW EX7 * 15 F1
Manor Steps BRIX TQ5 * 64 C2
Manor St DART TQ6 61 G5
Manor Ter BRIX TQ5 * 64 C2
PAIGN TQ3 2 C4
Manor Vale Rd BRIX TQ5 63 E2
Manor Vw NWTAB TQ12 23 E2
Manor Wy TOT TQ9 50 C3
Mansands La BRIX TQ5 69 F2
Mansbridge Rd TOT TQ9 51 E4
Manscombe Cl
SPH/CHEL/BTN TQ2 47 F3
Manscombe Rd
SPH/CHEL/BTN TQ2 47 F4
Maple Av BVYTR TQ13 10 A1
Maple Cl BRIX TQ5 64 A5
NWTAB TQ12 18 A5
Mapledene Cl TOT TQ9 56 D4
Maple Rd BRIX TQ5 64 A5
Mapletone Cl NWTAB TQ12 22 D1
Marcombe Rd
SPH/CHEL/BTN TQ2 4 A2
Mardle Wy BUCKF TQ11 34 C4
Margaret Gdns NWTAB TQ12 24 B2
Margaret Rd NWTAB TQ12 18 A3
NWTAB TQ12 22 D4
Marguerite Cl NWTAB TQ12 22 C1
Marguerite Wy NWTAB TQ12 31 G4
Marina Cl BRIX TQ5 65 E2
Marina Dr BRIX TQ5 65 E2
Marina Rd BRIX TQ5 65 E3
Marine Dr PAIGN TQ3 55 E2
Marine Gdns PAIGN TQ3 55 E1
Marine Pde DAW EX7 15 G2
PAIGN TQ3 55 F1
TEIGN TQ14 21 F5
Marine Pk PAIGN TQ3 55 E2
Mariners Wy PAIGN TQ3 46 B5
Marion Vw TQ TQ1 5 J4
Market Cl BUCKF TQ11 34 B4
Market Sq DART TQ6 71 F2
Market St BRIX TQ5 64 C2
BUCKF TQ11 34 C4
DART TQ6 71 F2
NWTAB TQ12 23 F2
SALC TQ8 77 F2
TQ TQ1 5 G2
The Market TQ TQ1 * 5 G2
Marlborough Av TQ TQ1 48 D1
Marldon Av PAIGN TQ3 2 C2
Marldon Cross Hl PAIGN TQ3 45 H3
Marldon Gv PAIGN TQ3 45 G3
Marldon La PAIGN TQ3 45 F2
Marldon Rd PAIGN TQ3 46 B5
Marldon Wy PAIGN TQ3 46 A3
Marnham Rd TQ TQ1 40 B4
Marsh Rd NWTAB TQ12 23 G2
Marston Cl DAW EX7 9 E5
Martinique Gv
SPH/CHEL/BTN TQ2 32 D5
Mary St BVYTR TQ13 7 E2
Mashford Av DART TQ6 70 C1
Mathill Cl BRIX TQ5 64 B4
Mathill Rd BRIX TQ5 64 B4
Matlock Ter
SPH/CHEL/BTN TQ2 * 5 F2
Maudlin Dr TEIGN TQ14 14 B5
Maudlin Rd TOT TQ9 50 C4
Mayfair Rd NWTAB TQ12 36 B1
Mayfield Crs NWTAB TQ12 22 D2
Mayflower Av NWTAB TQ12 24 B3
Mayflower Cl DART TQ6 70 D1
DAW EX7 15 G1
Mayflower Dr BRIX TQ5 64 C4
Mayor's Av DART TQ6 71 F2
Mead Cl PAIGN TQ3 54 D2
Meadfoot Cl TQ TQ1 49 F2
Meadfoot Cross TQ TQ1 5 K6
Meadfoot La TQ TQ1 5 J5
Meadfoot Rd TQ TQ1 5 J5
Meadfoot Sea Rd TQ TQ1 48 D3
Mead La PAIGN TQ3 54 D2
Meadow Cl NWTAB TQ12 31 F2
TOT TQ9 51 F4
Meadowcroft Dr NWTAB TQ12 17 H1
Meadow Halt NWTAB TQ12 23 E4
Meadow Pk BRIX TQ5 64 B2
DAW EX7 8 C5
PAIGN TQ3 45 H3
Meadow Ri DAW EX7 8 B5
TEIGN TQ14 20 D1
Meadow Rd
SPH/CHEL/BTN TQ2 4 A5
Meadowside NWTAB TQ12 23 E2
The Meadows NWTAB TQ12 18 B4
Meadow Vw NWTAB TQ12 22 D4
Mead Rd SPH/CHEL/BTN TQ2 47 F4
Meadway NWTAB TQ12 23 H5
Medway Rd
SPH/CHEL/BTN TQ2 40 B1
Melcot Cl NWTAB TQ12 18 A3
Meldrum Cl DAW EX7 15 G1
Mellows Meadow
NWTAB TQ12 22 D2
Melville La SPH/CHEL/BTN TQ2 5 G3
Melville Pl
SPH/CHEL/BTN TQ2 * 5 G3
Melville St SPH/CHEL/BTN TQ2 5 G3
Mena Park Cl GDRG/BDS TQ4 58 B2
Mendip Rd
SPH/CHEL/BTN TQ2 47 E3
Mere La TEIGN TQ14 21 G3
Merivale Cl TEIGN TQ14 21 G1
Merlin Wy SPH/CHEL/BTN TQ2 39 F1
Merrifield Rd BUCKF TQ11 34 A4
Merritt Rd PAIGN TQ3 2 C5
Merrivale Cl
SPH/CHEL/BTN TQ2 33 E4
Merryland Cl PAIGN TQ3 46 D4
Merryland Gdns PAIGN TQ3 46 D4
Merrywood NWTAB TQ12 22 D4
Metherell Av BRIX TQ5 64 C4
Mews Gdns DART TQ6 * 71 F2
The Mews DAW EX7 15 G2
Meyrick Rd TQ TQ1 40 C4
Middle Blagdon La PAIGN TQ3 53 F3
Middle Budleigh Meadow
NWTAB TQ12 22 D2
Middle Lincombe Rd TQ TQ1 48 D3
Middle Ramshill La PAIGN TQ3 53 G2
Middle St BRIX TQ5 64 C2
TEIGN TQ14 21 E5
Middle Warberry Rd TQ TQ1 5 J2
Midvale Rd GDRG/BDS TQ4 2 E4
Midway NWTAB TQ12 31 F2
Milber La NWTAB TQ12 31 G1
Mile End Rd NWTAB TQ12 16 C5
Milford Cl TEIGN TQ14 21 E3
Mill Bottom La NWTAB TQ12 26 A2
Millbrook Park Rd
SPH/CHEL/BTN TQ2 4 B1
Millbrook Rd PAIGN TQ3 2 E2
Mill Cl NWTAB TQ12 22 D1
Mill Crs DART TQ6 70 D1
Mill End NWTAB TQ12 13 E5
Millen La NWTAB TQ12 26 C3
Millers La TOT TQ9 56 C5
Mill Hl TOT TQ9 56 D5
Mill Hill Ct TOT TQ9 56 D5
Mill La BRIX TQ5 62 C3
BRIX TQ5 69 E1
NWTAB TQ12 22 B4
NWTAB TQ12 37 H1
PAIGN TQ3 2 E1
PAIGN TQ3 37 H2
SPH/CHEL/BTN TQ2 4 C1
TEIGN TQ14 20 D2
TOT TQ9 50 D4
Millmans Rd PAIGN TQ3 45 H3
Mill Pk NWTAB TQ12 * 12 D5
Mill St KING TQ7 75 E3
Mill Tail TOT TQ9 50 C4
Millwood BVYTR TQ13 10 A1
Milton Cl BRIX TQ5 64 B5
Milton Crs BRIX TQ5 64 B5
Milton Flds BRIX TQ5 64 A5
Milton La DART TQ6 70 C3
Milton Pk BRIX TQ5 64 A5
Milton Rd NWTAB TQ12 23 F1
Milton St BRIX TQ5 64 B5
Minacre La NWTAB TQ12 38 A2
Mincent Cl SPH/CHEL/BTN TQ2 33 E5
Mincent Hl
SPH/CHEL/BTN TQ2 33 E5
Minden Rd TEIGN TQ14 21 F3
Miners Cl BVYTR TQ13 29 G3
Minerva Wy NWTAB TQ12 24 A2
Miranda Rd PAIGN TQ3 54 B1
Mitre Cl TEIGN TQ14 19 G2
Moat Hl TOT TQ9 50 C5
Moles Cross PAIGN TQ3 38 A4
Moles La PAIGN TQ3 38 A3
Monastery Rd PAIGN TQ3 2 D3
Monksbridge Rd BRIX TQ5 64 B4
Monks Orch NWTAB TQ12 30 A1
Monks Wy BVYTR TQ13 7 E4
Monro Md NWTAB TQ12 10 A5
Montagu Cl KING TQ7 75 F2
Montagu Rd KING TQ7 74 D3
Monterey Cl
SPH/CHEL/BTN TQ2 4 A5
Montesson Cl PAIGN TQ3 53 H2
Montpellier Rd TQ TQ1 5 H4
Montserrat Ri
SPH/CHEL/BTN TQ2 32 C5
Moor Cl TEIGN TQ14 21 G1
Moore Cl NWTAB TQ12 24 B5
Moorhayes BVYTR TQ13 7 F3
Moorland Ga NWTAB TQ12 11 E3
Moorland Pk BVYTR TQ13 10 B1
Moorland Vw BUCKF TQ11 34 B4
NWTAB TQ12 24 B3
Moor La SPH/CHEL/BTN TQ2 33 E5
Moor Lane Cl
SPH/CHEL/BTN TQ2 33 E5
Moorpark Rd NWTAB TQ12 31 F2
Moor Rd TOT TQ9 42 B1
Moors End NWTAB TQ12 17 H3
Moorsend NWTAB TQ12 22 C1
Moors Pk TEIGN TQ14 19 H3
Moorstone Leat
GDRG/BDS TQ4 59 E3
Moorview PAIGN TQ3
Moorview Dr TEIGN TQ14
Moorview End PAIGN TQ3
Moretonhampstead Rd
BVYTR TQ13
Morgan Av
SPH/CHEL/BTN TQ2
Morin Rd PAIGN TQ3
Morningside DAW EX7
Mortimer Av PAIGN TQ3
Motehole Rd NWTAB TQ12
Moult Rd SALC TQ8
Mount Boone DART TQ6
Mount Boone Hl DART TQ6
Mount Boone La DART TQ6
Mount Boone Wy DART TQ6
Mount Hermon Rd TQ TQ1
Mount Pleasant DART TQ6 *
Mount Pleasant Cl KING TQ7
NWTAB TQ12
Mount Pleasant La
TEIGN TQ14
Mount Pleasant Rd BRIX TQ5
DAW EX7
NWTAB TQ12
NWTAB TQ12
TQ TQ1
Mount Ridley Rd DART TQ6
Mount Rd BRIX TQ5
The Mount BRIX TQ5 *
TEIGN TQ14
Mudstone La BRIX TQ5
Mulberry Cl PAIGN TQ3
Mulberry St TEIGN TQ14
Murley Crs TEIGN TQ14
Murley Gra TEIGN TQ14
Museum Rd TQ TQ1
Musket Rd NWTAB TQ12

N

Naida V DART TQ6
Naseby Dr NWTAB TQ12
Nash Gdns DAW EX7
Nelson Cl TEIGN TQ14
TOT TQ9
TQ TQ1
Nelson Pl NWTAB TQ12
Nelson Rd BRIX TQ5
DART TQ6
Ness Dr TEIGN TQ14
Ness View Rd TEIGN TQ14
Netherleigh Rd TQ TQ1
Nether Meadow PAIGN TQ3
Netley Rd NWTAB TQ12
Neville Rd NWTAB TQ12
Newcross Pk NWTAB TQ12
Newhay Cl DAW EX7
Newlands DAW EX7
Newlands Dr BVYTR TQ13
New Park Cl BRIX TQ5
New Park Rd NWTAB TQ12
PAIGN TQ3
Newport St DART TQ6
New Quay La BRIX TQ5
New Quay St TEIGN TQ14
New Rd BRIX TQ5
BUCKF TQ11
TEIGN TQ14
TOT TQ9
TOT TQ9
New St PAIGN TQ3
Newtake Mt NWTAB TQ12 *
Newtake Ri NWTAB TQ12
Newton Hl NWTAB TQ12
Newton Rd BVYTR TQ13
NWTAB TQ12
NWTAB TQ12
SALC TQ8
SPH/CHEL/BTN TQ2
TEIGN TQ14
New Wk TOT TQ9
Nicholson Rd
SPH/CHEL/BTN TQ2
Nightingale Cl
SPH/CHEL/BTN TQ2
Noelle Dr NWTAB TQ12
Norden La KING TQ7
Norman Cl NWTAB TQ12
Norman Rd PAIGN TQ3
North Boundary Rd BRIX TQ5
North Emb DART TQ6
North End Cl NWTAB TQ12
Northfields La BRIX TQ5
Northfields Rd BRIX TQ5
North Ford Rd DART TQ6
North Furzeham Rd BRIX TQ5
North Hill Cl BRIX TQ5
Northleat Av PAIGN TQ3
North Lodge Cl DAW EX7
North Quay GDRG/BDS TQ4 *
North Rocks Rd
GDRG/BDS TQ4
North St BVYTR TQ13
NWTAB TQ12
TOT TQ9
Northumberland Pl
TEIGN TQ14
North View Rd BRIX TQ5
Northville Pk KING TQ7
Northville Rd KING TQ7
Northwood La BUCKF TQ11
Nursery Cl PAIGN TQ3
Nursery Rd NWTAB TQ12
Nut Bush La
SPH/CHEL/BTN TQ2
Nut Tree Orch BRIX TQ5

O

Oakbank BVYTR TQ13
Oak Cl NWTAB TQ12
Oak Hl DAW EX7
Oak Hill Cross Rd TEIGN TQ14

l Rd *TQ* TQ1 39 H5
nd Cl *DART* TQ6 70 C3
nd Dr *DAW* EX7 15 F2
nd Rd *NWTAB* TQ12 24 B3
nds Pk *BUCKF* TQ11 34 B4
nds Rd *BUCKF* TQ11 34 A3
wn *NWTAB* TQ12 23 G3
wn Ter *TQ* TQ1 * 39 H4
Cl *KING* TQ7 75 E4
Pk *NWTAB* TQ12 10 C5
Cl *TEIGN* TQ14 21 F1
ark Av
/*CHEL/BTN* TQ2 39 F3
ark Cl
/*CHEL/BTN* TQ2 39 F3
ark Rd *DAW* EX7 8 D5
TAB TQ12 22 D1
aks *BVYTR* TQ13 7 G3
ee Dr *NWTAB* TQ12 24 B5
ee Gv *TEIGN* TQ14 21 E5
ee Yd *PAIGN* TQ3 * 55 E1
ds Dr *GDRG/BDS* TQ4 2 C7
nbe Valley Rd
GN TQ3 46 C4
View Crs *BRIX* TQ5 69 E1
View Dr *BRIX* TQ5 69 E1
Gv *TQ* TQ1 39 G4
ombe Beach Hl
TQ1 40 D3
ll Gv *NWTAB* TQ12 30 A2
l End Dr *NWTAB* TQ12 22 D4
l Mill Rd *NWTAB* TQ12 22 C3
l Rd *NWTAB* TQ12 22 C5
r Cl *PAIGN* TQ3 46 B4
der Works La
TAB TQ12 30 A1
ourg Pk *PAIGN* TQ3 3 G1
eter Rd *NWTAB* TQ12 23 F1
rm Wy *DAW* EX7 15 F3
tehouse Rd *DAW* EX7 8 D5
anor Cl *BVYTR* TQ13 28 D2
ll La *DART* TQ6 70 D1
ll Rd
/*CHEL/BTN* TQ2 4 A5
ewton Rd *NWTAB* TQ12 10 C1
TAB TQ12 31 E2
ch *BVYTR* TQ13 7 F3
aignton La *PAIGN* TQ3 47 F5
aignton Rd
/*CHEL/BTN* TQ2 47 F3
ay St *TEIGN* TQ14 21 F4
BRIX TQ5 62 D2
gnmouth Rd *DAW* EX7 15 F3
rquay Rd *PAIGN* TQ3 55 E1
rwood Rd *TQ* TQ1 5 K3
tnes Rd *BUCKF* TQ11 34 D4
TR TQ13 29 E5
TAB TQ12 23 E4
wn St *DAW* EX7 15 E1
alls Hl *TEIGN* TQ14 20 A1
y Rd *PAIGN* TQ3 54 D1
iddicombe La
GN TQ3 53 H3
iddicombe Rd
GN TQ3 53 F1
iddicome La *PAIGN* TQ3 53 E1
oods Hl
/*CHEL/BTN* TQ2 39 G4
Gdns *DAW* EX7 9 G2
y *DAW* EX7 9 G2
w Rd *SALC* TQ8 77 E2
e Gv
/*CHEL/BTN* TQ2 39 H1
rd Cl *BRIX* TQ5 62 D2
X TQ5 64 C4
V EX7 15 F1
TAB TQ12 12 D4
TAB TQ12 22 B4
GN TQ14 20 C5
rd Dr *NWTAB* TQ12 31 F4
TAB TQ12 36 B1
rd Gdns *DAW* EX7 15 F1
GN TQ14 21 G4
rd Gv *BRIX* TQ5 64 C5
rd Pk *DART* TQ6 * 61 G4
rd Rd
/*CHEL/BTN* TQ2 39 H2
rchards *BRIX* TQ5 62 D2
rd Ter *DART* TQ6 * 71 H2
TAB TQ12 30 B1
rchard *DAW* EX7 15 E5
GN TQ14 19 H2
TQ9 * 50 C4
rd View Wear Farm
GN TQ14 * 19 E3
rd Wy *TOT* TQ9 56 D4
rd Waye *TOT* TQ9 50 B4
Av *NWTAB* TQ12 17 H3
V *NWTAB* TQ12 18 A1
one Dr *TQ* TQ1 33 G3
one La
/*CHEL/BTN* TQ2 32 C5
Rd *PAIGN* TQ3 47 F5
y Cl
/*CHEL/BTN* TQ2 39 G1
h Av *NWTAB* TQ12 17 F5
h Pk *NWTAB* TQ12 17 F5
n Rd *PAIGN* TQ3 46 C4
n Cl *NWTAB* TQ12 36 B1
ne St *NWTAB* TQ12 23 H2
nd's La *TEIGN* TQ14 21 F4
Av *GDRG/BDS* TQ4 2 E6
Crs *GDRG/BDS* TQ4 2 E6
Gdns
RG/BDS TQ4 2 E6
Rd
/*CHEL/BTN* TQ2 39 E4
lose *PAIGN* TQ3 54 A1
ale Cl
/*CHEL/BTN* TQ2 32 D4
ang *BRIX* TQ5 64 D2
ang Rd *BRIX* TQ5 64 C1
ill *DART* TQ6 * 71 H2
d La *BRIX* TQ5 64 A3
d St *DART* TQ6 71 F2
Cl *TQ* TQ1 49 E2
Rd
TQ1 49 E2
r Bend *GDRG/BDS* TQ4 59 E2
r Cl *GDRG/BDS* TQ4 59 E2

P

Packhall La *BRIX* TQ5 64 A5
Padacre Rd
SPH/CHEL/BTN TQ2 33 E5
The Paddocks *NWTAB* TQ12 30 B1
TOT TQ9 * 50 D3
The Paddock *BRIX* TQ5 64 B3
DAW EX7 8 C5
Paddons Coombe
NWTAB TQ12 18 A1
Paddons La *TEIGN* TQ14 21 E1
Pafford Cl *SPH/CHEL/BTN* TQ2 40 A1
Paige Adams Rd *TOT* TQ9 50 B3
Paignton Rd *TOT* TQ9 56 D4
Painton Ms *GDRG/BDS* TQ4 2 E4
Palace Av *PAIGN* TQ3 2 E3
Palace Pl *PAIGN* TQ3 2 E2
Palatine Cl *TQ* TQ1 5 H2
Palermo Rd *TQ* TQ1 40 C4
Palk Cl *TEIGN* TQ14 20 D5
Palk St *SPH/CHEL/BTN* TQ2 5 H5
Palm Ct *DAW* EX7 9 F2
Palm Rd *SPH/CHEL/BTN* TQ2 4 E1
The Palms *TQ* TQ1 * 48 D2
Paradise Gln *TEIGN* TQ14 21 F2
Paradise Pl *BRIX* TQ5 64 D2
Paradise Rd *TEIGN* TQ14 21 F2
Paris Rd *PAIGN* TQ3 55 E1
Park Av *BRIX* TQ5 64 B4
Parkelands *BVYTR* TQ13 7 E3
Parkers Cl *TOT* TQ9 50 D5
Parkers Wy *TOT* TQ9 50 D4
Parkfield Cl *PAIGN* TQ3 45 H3
TOT TQ9 51 F4
Parkfield Rd *TQ* TQ1 39 H4
Parkham Gld *BRIX* TQ5 64 C3
Parkham La *BRIX* TQ5 64 C3
Parkham Rd *BRIX* TQ5 64 C3
Park Hl *TEIGN* TQ14 21 F4
Parkhill Rd *TQ* TQ1 5 H6
Parkhurst Rd *TQ* TQ1 39 H4
Parklands *TOT* TQ9 50 D3
Parklands Wy *BVYTR* TQ13 10 A1
Park La *TQ* TQ1 5 H5
Park Ms *BRIX* TQ5 65 E2
Park Ri *DAW* EX7 15 F3
SALC TQ8 77 E3
Park Rd *DAW* EX7 15 F1
NWTAB TQ12 31 F3
TOT TQ9 42 C4
TQ TQ1 40 B2
Parkside Rd *GDRG/BDS* TQ4 3 G3
Park Vw *NWTAB* TQ12 24 B5
Parsonage La *TOT* TQ9 43 E3
Parson St *TEIGN* TQ14 21 F3
Paternoster La *NWTAB* TQ12 36 A1
Pathfields *TOT* TQ9 50 D4
Pavor Rd *SPH/CHEL/BTN* TQ2 40 B1
Paynsford Rd *NWTAB* TQ12 23 F1
Peak Tor Av *TQ* TQ1 5 K7
Peaseditch *BRIX* TQ5 64 D4
Peasland Rd
SPH/CHEL/BTN TQ2 33 E4
Pebble Ct *GDRG/BDS* TQ4 3 F7
Pegwell La *TEIGN* TQ14 26 B2
Pellew Ar *TEIGN* TQ14 * 21 F4
Pellew Wy *TEIGN* TQ14 21 E1
Pembroke Pk *PAIGN* TQ3 46 A3
Pembroke Rd *PAIGN* TQ3 54 A2
TQ TQ1 5 H1
Pencorse Rd
SPH/CHEL/BTN TQ2 39 H3
Pendennis Rd
SPH/CHEL/BTN TQ2 39 H3
Penfield Gdns *DAW* EX7 15 E1
Penhill La *BRIX* TQ5 68 C2
Pennine Dr *GDRG/BDS* TQ4 53 H5
Penn Inn Cl *NWTAB* TQ12 24 A3
Penn La *BRIX* TQ5 64 C4
Penn Mdw *BRIX* TQ5 64 D4
Penn Meadows Cl *BRIX* TQ5 64 D3
Pennsylvania Rd *TQ* TQ1 5 H2
Pennyacre Rd *TEIGN* TQ14 21 G2
Penpethy Cl *BRIX* TQ5 64 B3
Penpethy Rd *BRIX* TQ5 64 B3
Penrhyn Pl *TEIGN* TQ14 * 21 E5
Penryn Pl *TEIGN* TQ14 21 E5
Penshurst Rd *NWTAB* TQ12 23 F4
Pensilva Pk *BRIX* TQ5 64 C5
Pentridge Av
SPH/CHEL/BTN TQ2 47 E4
Penwill Wy *GDRG/BDS* TQ4 2 D7
Pepper La *DART* TQ6 72 C1
Peppery La *TEIGN* TQ14 20 D5
Peregrine Cl
SPH/CHEL/BTN TQ2 32 B5
Perinville Cl *TQ* TQ1 41 E5
Perinville Rd *TQ* TQ1 40 D4
Perros Cl *TEIGN* TQ14 20 D2
Perry La *NWTAB* TQ12 16 A4
Peters Crs *PAIGN* TQ3 45 H3
Petitor Ms *TQ* TQ1 40 B2
Petitor Rd *TQ* TQ1 40 C2
Petit Well La *TQ* TQ1 40 B2
Petrel Cl *SPH/CHEL/BTN* TQ2 32 A5
Petroc Dr *NWTAB* TQ12 23 G1
Picket Head Hl *TEIGN* TQ14 27 E1
Piermont Pl *DAW* EX7 15 G1
Pillar Av *BRIX* TQ5 64 B2
Pillar Cl *BRIX* TQ5 64 B2
Pillar Crs *BRIX* TQ5 64 B2
Pilmuir Av *SPH/CHEL/BTN* TQ2 4 B1
Pimlico *TQ* TQ1 5 G2
Pimm Rd *PAIGN* TQ3 54 A2
Pine Cl *BRIX* TQ5 64 B5
TEIGN TQ14 21 H1
Pines Rd *PAIGN* TQ3 54 A1
Pine Tree Cl *DAW* EX7 9 G2
Pine View Gdns *TQ* TQ1 40 C5
Pinewood Cl *DAW* EX7 9 F4
Pitcairn Cresent
SPH/CHEL/BTN TQ2 32 C5
Pitland La *NWTAB* TQ12 32 C3
Pitley Rd *BVYTR* TQ13 29 H3
Pitt Hill Rd *NWTAB* TQ12 16 D5
Place La *BVYTR* TQ13 29 G2
Plainmoor Rd *TQ* TQ1 40 B4
The Plains *DART* TQ6 * 71 G2
TOT TQ9 50 D4
Plantation Ter *DAW* EX7 15 F1
Plantation Wy
SPH/CHEL/BTN TQ2 39 E1
Platt Cl *SALC* TQ8 76 D3
Platway La *TEIGN* TQ14 20 D5
Pleasant Ter *PAIGN* TQ3 * 2 D2
Pleases Pas *TOT* TQ9 * 50 C4
Plym Cl *SPH/CHEL/BTN* TQ2 38 D4
Plymouth Rd *BUCKF* TQ11 34 C5
KING TQ7 74 D1
TOT TQ9 50 A4
Polhearne La *BRIX* TQ5 64 B4
Polhearne Wy *BRIX* TQ5 64 B4
Polsham Pk *PAIGN* TQ3 3 F1
Pomeroy Av *BRIX* TQ5 64 A2
Pomeroy Pl *NWTAB* TQ12 10 A5
Pomeroy Rd *NWTAB* TQ12 23 E2
Pooks La *BVYTR* TQ13 29 F3
Pools Wier *NWTAB* TQ12 26 B5
Poplar *DAW* EX7 9 F2
Poplar Cl *BRIX* TQ5 68 D1
NWTAB TQ12 24 C5
Poplar Dr *KING* TQ7 75 E3
Poplars Dr *PAIGN* TQ3 45 H4
Porlock Wy *GDRG/BDS* TQ4 58 B2
Portland Av *TEIGN* TQ14 21 G1
Portland Rd *TQ* TQ1 40 D4
Potters Hl *TQ* TQ1 5 G1
Pottery Ms
SPH/CHEL/BTN TQ2 * 4 D1
Pottery Rd *BVYTR* TQ13 7 E5
NWTAB TQ12 17 H5
Pound Fld *TOT* TQ9 56 D4
Pound La *NWTAB* TQ12 31 F4
TEIGN TQ14 20 C5
Pound Pl *NWTAB* TQ12 23 F2
Poundsgate Cl *BRIX* TQ5 65 E3
Powderham Cl *NWTAB* TQ12 23 F3
Powderham Rd
SPH/CHEL/BTN TQ2 39 H2
NWTAB TQ12 23 F2
Powderham Ter *TEIGN* TQ14 21 G5
The Precinct *KING* TQ7 75 E2
Prestbury Pk
SPH/CHEL/BTN TQ2 * 4 C1
Preston Down Av *PAIGN* TQ3 46 D4
Preston Down Rd *PAIGN* TQ3 46 A3
SPH/CHEL/BTN TQ2 39 E5
Prigg Meadow *BVYTR* TQ13 29 F4
Primley Ct *PAIGN* TQ3 54 A4
Primley Pk *PAIGN* TQ3 2 B4
Primley Pk East *PAIGN* TQ3 2 D4
Primrose Wy *NWTAB* TQ12 31 F2
Prince Albert Pl *DAW* EX7 * 15 F1
Prince Charles Ct
SPH/CHEL/BTN TQ2 33 E5
Prince of Wales Dr *DART* TQ6 71 F1
Prince Rupert Wy
NWTAB TQ12 11 E3
Princes Point *TQ* TQ1 * 5 J6
Princes Rd *TQ* TQ1 5 H1
Princes Rd East *TQ* TQ1 5 K1
Princes Rd West *TQ* TQ1 5 H1
Princess Rd *NWTAB* TQ12 17 H2
NWTAB TQ12 31 G4
Princes St *PAIGN* TQ3 2 E2
TQ TQ1 40 D4
Prince St *NWTAB* TQ12 23 G2
Priory *BVYTR* TQ13 7 E2
Priory Av *NWTAB* TQ12 31 G3
TOT TQ9 50 C3
Priory Dr *TOT* TQ9 50 C3
Priory Hl *DAW* EX7 15 G1
TOT TQ9 50 C3
Priory Park Rd *DAW* EX7 15 F1
Priory Rd *DAW* EX7 15 G1
NWTAB TQ12 30 C1
TQ TQ1 40 B3
Priscott Wy *NWTAB* TQ12 18 A4
Promenade *GDRG/BDS* TQ4 3 H7
KING TQ7 75 F3
PAIGN TQ3 55 F1
Prospect Rd *BRIX* TQ5 64 C2
Prospect Steps *BRIX* TQ5 * 64 C2
Prospect Ter *NWTAB* TQ12 23 G2
Pump St *BRIX* TQ5 64 D2
Purbeck Av
SPH/CHEL/BTN TQ2 47 E4

Q

Quantocks Rd
SPH/CHEL/BTN TQ2 47 E3
Quarry Gdns *PAIGN* TQ3 54 C2
Quay Rd *NWTAB* TQ12 23 H2
TEIGN TQ14 21 F4
Quay Ter *NWTAB* TQ12 23 H2
The Quay *BRIX* TQ5 64 D2
DART TQ6 61 H5
DART TQ6 71 F2
Queen Elizabeth Av
DART TQ6 71 E1
Queen Elizabeth Dr
PAIGN TQ3 54 A3
Queen La *DAW* EX7 15 F1
Queens Cl *NWTAB* TQ12 18 B2
Queen's Crs *BRIX* TQ5 64 D4
Queen's Park Rd
GDRG/BDS TQ4 3 G3
Queen's Rd *BRIX* TQ5 64 C1
GDRG/BDS TQ4 3 G4
Queens Steps *BRIX* TQ5 * 64 D2
Queen St *DAW* EX7 15 F1
NWTAB TQ12 23 G2
TEIGN TQ14 21 F4
TQ TQ1 5 G2
Queensway *NWTAB* TQ12 24 A3
SPH/CHEL/BTN TQ2 39 F5
Queensway Cl
SPH/CHEL/BTN TQ2 39 G4
Queensway Crs
SPH/CHEL/BTN TQ2 39 G4
Quentin Av *BRIX* TQ5 64 B5
Quinta Cl *TQ* TQ1 40 C5
Quinta Rd *TQ* TQ1 40 C5

R

Rack Park Rd *KING* TQ7 75 F3
Raddicombe Cl *BRIX* TQ5 68 D2
Raddicombe Dr *BRIX* TQ5 68 D2
Radway Ct *TEIGN* TQ14 20 A1
Radway Gdns *TEIGN* TQ14 20 A2
Radway Hl *TEIGN* TQ14 20 A2
Radway St *TEIGN* TQ14 20 A2
Raleigh Av *SPH/CHEL/BTN* TQ2 39 F5
Raleigh Cl *DART* TQ6 70 C2
Raleigh Dr *GDRG/BDS* TQ4 58 D2
Raleigh Rd *DART* TQ6 71 E1
NWTAB TQ12 24 B2
SALC TQ8 77 E3
TEIGN TQ14 21 E1
Ramshill Rd *PAIGN* TQ3 54 A1
Randolph Ct *NWTAB* TQ12 23 E1
Rangers Cl *BUCKF* TQ11 34 C5
Ranscombe Cl *BRIX* TQ5 65 E2
Ranscombe Rd *BRIX* TQ5 64 D2
Rathmore Rd
SPH/CHEL/BTN TQ2 4 C4
Rawlyn Rd
SPH/CHEL/BTN TQ2 47 F2
Rea Barn Cl *BRIX* TQ5 64 D3
Rea Barn Rd *BRIX* TQ5 64 D3
Rea Dr *BRIX* TQ5 64 D2
Rectory Rd *NWTAB* TQ12 22 C5
Redavon Ri
SPH/CHEL/BTN TQ2 38 D3
Red Brook Cl *GDRG/BDS* TQ4 59 E3
Redburn Cl *PAIGN* TQ3 2 D1
Redburn Rd *PAIGN* TQ3 2 D1
Redcliffe Rd *TQ* TQ1 40 C2
Reddenhill Rd *TQ* TQ1 40 C5
Redford Wy *KING* TQ7 75 E3
Redgate Cl *TQ* TQ1 40 D5
Redlands Ct *PAIGN* TQ3 54 A2
Redlap Rd *DART* TQ6 70 D5
Redoubt Hl *DART* TQ6 71 G2
Redwell La *PAIGN* TQ3 54 B1
Redwell Rd *PAIGN* TQ3 54 B1
Redwood Cl *BVYTR* TQ13 10 A1
Redwoods *BVYTR* TQ13 7 E5
Reed V *TEIGN* TQ14 21 E3
Reeves Cl *TOT* TQ9 * 50 D4
The Reeves Rd
SPH/CHEL/BTN TQ2 47 F1
Regent Cl *SPH/CHEL/BTN* TQ2 39 G3
Regent St *DAW* EX7 15 F1
TEIGN TQ14 21 G4
Rendells Meadow *BVYTR* TQ13 7 G3
Reservoir Ter *DART* TQ6 * 71 H2
Retreat Cl *KING* TQ7 75 E3
The Retreat *NWTAB* TQ12 * 23 F2
PAIGN TQ3 55 E1
Rew Rd *BVYTR* TQ13 29 F2
Reynell Av *NWTAB* TQ12 24 B2
Reynell Rd *NWTAB* TQ12 22 D5
Rhine Vls *TOT* TQ9 * 50 D4
Rhodanthe Rd *PAIGN* TQ3 46 D5
Richards Cl *DAW* EX7 15 E2
Richmond Cl *TQ* TQ1 49 G1
Richmond Ct *PAIGN* TQ3 54 D1
Richmond Hl *NWTAB* TQ12 31 G3
Ridge Hl *DART* TQ6 71 F1
Ridge La *NWTAB* TQ12 38 B3
Ridgemark Cl *BRIX* TQ5 65 E2
Ridge Rd *NWTAB* TQ12 25 F3
TQ TQ1 33 F2
The Ridges *DART* TQ6 70 D3
Ridgeway Cl *NWTAB* TQ12 24 B4
Ridgeway Hl *PAIGN* TQ3 37 H5
Ridgeway La *NWTAB* TQ12 32 A2
Ridgeway Rd *NWTAB* TQ12 24 B4
TQ TQ1 48 D3
Ridley Hl *DART* TQ6 71 G2
Rillage La *SPH/CHEL/BTN* TQ2 39 H5
Ringmore Cl *TEIGN* TQ14 20 D5
Ringmore Rd *TEIGN* TQ14 20 D5
Ringslade Cl *NWTAB* TQ12 16 D5
Ringslade Rd *NWTAB* TQ12 16 D4
Rippon Cl *BRIX* TQ5 63 H5
Riverside *TEIGN* TQ14 21 E5
TOT TQ9 50 B2
Riverside Rd *DART* TQ6 61 G4
River Vw *DART* TQ6 * 71 G2
Riverview *NWTAB* TQ12 24 B3
The Riviera *GDRG/BDS* TQ4 3 F5
TQ TQ1 * 5 J5
Riviera Wy
SPH/CHEL/BTN TQ2 39 E2
Robers Rd *NWTAB* TQ12 17 H2
Roberts Cl *SPH/CHEL/BTN* TQ2 40 B1
Roberts Wy *NWTAB* TQ12 22 D1
Roborough La *BVYTR* TQ13 29 F3
Rock Cl *GDRG/BDS* TQ4 59 E5
Rock End Av *TQ* TQ1 5 K7
Rockfield Cl *TEIGN* TQ14 21 H1
Rock House La *TQ* TQ1 33 G4
Rocklands Ter *BRIX* TQ5 * 64 C2
Rock Pk *DART* TQ6 70 D1
Rock Rd *SPH/CHEL/BTN* TQ2 5 G3
The Rockstone *DAW* EX7 9 E5
Rocky La *TEIGN* TQ14 21 E2
Rocombe Cl
SPH/CHEL/BTN TQ2 32 D4
Rodney Cl *DART* TQ6 70 D2
Romaleyn Gdns
GDRG/BDS TQ4 * 3 F6
Ropewalk *KING* TQ7 75 E4
NWTAB TQ12 * 23 G2
Rope Wk *TEIGN* TQ14 21 F3
Ropewalk Hl *BRIX* TQ5 64 C2
Rose Dene
SPH/CHEL/BTN TQ2 39 H1
Rose Hl *NWTAB* TQ12 31 F4
Rosehill Cl *TQ* TQ1 5 J1
Rosehill Gdns *NWTAB* TQ12 31 F4
Rosehill Rd *TQ* TQ1 5 H1
Roselands Dr *GDRG/BDS* TQ4 58 A1
Roselands Rd *GDRG/BDS* TQ4 58 C2
Rosemary Gdns *PAIGN* TQ3 54 B1
Rosery Rd *SPH/CHEL/BTN* TQ2 4 B2
Roseville St *DART* TQ6 71 F2
Rosewarne Av *NWTAB* TQ12 24 B3
Rossall Dr *PAIGN* TQ3 2 C4
Rosyl Av *DAW* EX7 15 E4
Rougemont Av
SPH/CHEL/BTN TQ2 39 E2
Round Berry Dr *SALC* TQ8 77 E3
Roundham Av *GDRG/BDS* TQ4 3 J6
Roundham Crs *GDRG/BDS* TQ4 3 H5
Roundham Gdns
GDRG/BDS TQ4 3 H6
Roundham Rd *GDRG/BDS* TQ4 3 H4
Roundhead Rd *NWTAB* TQ12 10 D2
Roundhill Rd
SPH/CHEL/BTN TQ2 47 F4
The Roundings *BRIX* TQ5 62 D2
Roundmoors Cl *NWTAB* TQ12 38 C1
The Roundway *NWTAB* TQ12 31 F3
Rousdown Rd
SPH/CHEL/BTN TQ2 4 B3
Rowan Cl *NWTAB* TQ12 22 D5
Rowantree Rd *NWTAB* TQ12 24 A4
Rowan Wy *BRIX* TQ5 69 E1
Rowbrook Cl *GDRG/BDS* TQ4 58 A1
Rowcroft Rd *PAIGN* TQ3 55 E1
Rowdens Rd
SPH/CHEL/BTN TQ2 4 C1
The Rowdens *TEIGN* TQ14 21 G2
Rowells Md *NWTAB* TQ12 10 A5
Rowley Rd *TQ* TQ1 40 C3
Rowsell's La *TOT* TQ9 50 D4
Ruckamore Rd
SPH/CHEL/BTN TQ2 4 A2
Rundle Rd *NWTAB* TQ12 23 G1
Rushlade Cl *GDRG/BDS* TQ4 58 B2
Rush Wy *TOT* TQ9 51 F4
Russets La *BUCKF* TQ11 34 D4
Ryde Cl *SPH/CHEL/BTN* TQ2 40 A1
Rydon Acres *NWTAB* TQ12 18 A2
TOT TQ9 56 D4
Rydon Av *NWTAB* TQ12 18 A2
Rydon Est *NWTAB* TQ12 18 A2
Rydon La *NWTAB* TQ12 30 C2
Rydon Rd *NWTAB* TQ12 18 A2
Rydons *BRIX* TQ5 64 A3

S

Sabre Cl *NWTAB* TQ12 10 C2
The Saddle *GDRG/BDS* TQ4 59 E2
Saffron Pk *KING* TQ7 75 F3
St Agnes La
SPH/CHEL/BTN TQ2 4 B5
St Albans Rd *TQ* TQ1 40 C4
St Andrews Rd *GDRG/BDS* TQ4 3 G4
St Annes Ct *NWTAB* TQ12 23 E2
St Anne's Rd *TQ* TQ1 40 C4
St Augustines Cl
SPH/CHEL/BTN TQ2 33 E5
St Bernard's Cl *BUCKF* TQ11 34 C2
St Columbia Cl *NWTAB* TQ12 18 A2
St David's Rd *TEIGN* TQ14 14 B5
St Dominic's Cl *TQ* TQ1 40 B3
St Dunstan's Rd *SALC* TQ8 77 E3
St Edmunds Rd *KING* TQ7 75 E2
St Edmund's Rd *TQ* TQ1 40 B4
St Efride's Rd
SPH/CHEL/BTN TQ2 4 D1
St Georges Cresent *TQ* TQ1 40 C4
St George's Rd *TQ* TQ1 40 C4
St James Pl *TQ* TQ1 40 D4
St James Rd *TQ* TQ1 40 A4
St John's Cl *TEIGN* TQ14 19 H3
St John's La *BVYTR* TQ13 7 E3
St Johns Pl *TQ* TQ1 5 H4
St John's St *NWTAB* TQ12 23 H1
St John's Ter *TOT* TQ9 50 B3
St Katharine's Rd *TQ* TQ1 39 G5
St Katherines Ms *TOT* TQ9 * 50 C4
St Katherine's Wy *TOT* TQ9 50 C4
St Kitts Cl *SPH/CHEL/BTN* TQ2 39 H1
St Lawrence La *BVYTR* TQ13 29 F4
St Leonard's Cl *NWTAB* TQ12 23 F2
St Leonard's Rd *NWTAB* TQ12 23 F2
St Luke's Cl *NWTAB* TQ12 24 B4
St Lukes Pk
SPH/CHEL/BTN TQ2 5 F3
St Luke's Rd *NWTAB* TQ12 24 A4
St Lukes Rd
SPH/CHEL/BTN TQ2 5 F3
St Lukes Rd North
SPH/CHEL/BTN TQ2 5 F3
St Lukes Rd South
SPH/CHEL/BTN TQ2 5 F3
St Marco Gdns *KING* TQ7 75 F2
St Margaret's Av *TQ* TQ1 40 B4
St Margaret's Cl *TQ* TQ1 40 B3
St Margaret's Rd *TQ* TQ1 40 B3
St Mark's Rd *TQ* TQ1 5 K6
St Marychurch Rd
NWTAB TQ12 24 B4
SPH/CHEL/BTN TQ2 39 G4
TQ TQ1 40 A5
St Mary's Cl *BRIX* TQ5 64 C5
St Marys Cl *NWTAB* TQ12 30 A2
St Marys Hl *BRIX* TQ5 64 D4
St Mary's Pk *GDRG/BDS* TQ4 53 G5
St Mary's Rd *BRIX* TQ5 64 C5
NWTAB TQ12 23 F3
TEIGN TQ14 21 E1
St Marys Sq *BRIX* TQ5 * 64 B4
St Matthew's Rd
SPH/CHEL/BTN TQ2 47 F2
St Matthias Church Rd *TQ* TQ1 49 E1
St Mawes Dr *GDRG/BDS* TQ4 58 D4
St Michael's Rd
GDRG/BDS TQ4 2 D5
St Michaels Rd *NWTAB* TQ12 17 H4
TEIGN TQ14 21 G1
St Michael's Rd *TQ* TQ1 39 G4
St Michaels Ter *TQ* TQ1 * 5 G1
St Patrick's Cl *TEIGN* TQ14 21 E2
St Pauls Cl *BVYTR* TQ13 7 F3
St Paul's Crs *TQ* TQ1 40 B4
St Paul's Rd *NWTAB* TQ12 23 G2
PAIGN TQ3 47 F5
TQ TQ1 40 B4
St Peter's Cl *BVYTR* TQ13 7 G2
St Peters Cl
SPH/CHEL/BTN TQ2 39 F5

W

dex - featured places

Acknowledgements

Schools address data provided by Education Direct.

Petrol station information supplied by Johnsons.

Garden centre information provided by:

Garden Centre Association ⚙ Britains best garden centres

Wyevale Garden Centres 🥦

The statement on the front cover of this atlas is sourced, selected and quoted from a reader comment and feedback form received in 2004